PRICING FOR RESULTS

John Winkler

Facts On File Publications
New York, New York ● Bicester, England

Pricing for Results

Originally published in 1983 by William Heinemann, Ltd., in conjunction with the Institute of Marketing.

Library of Congress Cataloging in Publication Data

Winkler, John.
    Pricing for results.

    Bibliography: p.
    Includes index.
    1. Price policy. I. Title.
HF5416.5.W56 1984   338.5'21   83-20630
ISBN 0-87196-849-5

Printed in United States of America

10 9 8 7 6 5 4 3 2 1

To the stars among my competitors—Aubrey Wilson who taught me how to lead seminars, John May who taught me presentation, Dan Nimer who taught me pricing, Bob Whitney who taught me how to position subjects. And to Heinz Goldmann who showed everyone how to become a star.

Contents

Introduction

I believe in market research.

Our research shows us that most managers do not buy many books on management. That will not surprise anyone.

But our research also shows that among those managers who do buy management books, very few managers read them in any depth. What they do, for the most part is to dip into them, select the bits they want, and then put the book in the office bookcase.

This book has three objectives. First, it is for the student who is desperately searching U.S. and British management libraries for a book that tells him how to base his prices on what the market will bear. I have not found another one. Management students read books, because the examination syllabus makes them.

Second, for the practicing manager it has been written according to the results of research telling us what he wants in a book if he is to do more than dip into it. He says he wants it to be readable. We have researched readers' reactions to the open, nonacademic style, we have researched their views on the forced choice questions, on the use of case examples, on the small hints and tips—we have even researched the basis of the title.

Thirdly, the book is designed to address itself to the most difficult pricing questions of the day about which there is a sore lack of appropriate theory. What are the issues of the day? Price wars, how to minimize the damage they do, how to stop them, when to start them. These are issues of the day. You will not have read another book about handling the price war.

The notion of morality in pricing decisions and how it affects business performance is another issue you will not have seen anyone touch.

Whether to allow your sales force to have discretion over setting your company's discounts; how to handle a discount battle; how to negotiate prices— these are relevant matters for the practicing manager.

In a world that is steadily using up its resources at a rate faster than the rate at which they are being replaced, this book devotes itself to the issue that will inevitably become one of the higher things in life—price.

Instant pricing | 1

The world is full of convenience products: instant meals, instant money, instant information, instant travel.

This chapter represents the world's first instant management consultancy. If you haven't got enough time to read the book, then commit this chapter to heart. Just add water, in a glass with a little whisky.

DEVELOP YOUR POWER

Whatever your sector of the market, be important in it. This is a book about pricing, so follow the old rule: "the strongest dictate the terms."

Become big in your sector of the market, but not at any price. You will get there by offering something new that people want, before most of the others offer it; by continually making what you offer better; and by marketing it forcefully, dedicating yourself to its success without compromise and by pricing it a bit above the average. That is the way to become market leader; you will not get there by giving it all away with lowest prices.

If you cannot be the biggest in the market, then take a smaller sector of it and be the best. Everything that you do, you must do well; your offerings must be superb in quality and finish. You must price them at a premium and market them hard. You will not be the biggest or the richest, but you will make a very comfortable living out of being a specialist.

WORK THE MARKET

Use your costs to give you the bottom line only. Don't use costs alone to set prices. How will costs tell you what the market will bear? Working the market means finding the soft areas where your prices are easier to obtain—normally to be found in the upper quality end, and from the direct customers you serve without going through middlemen, from customers who have money—how can you get your prices if your customers don't have the money? Go behind the professional buyer, because he knows how to get your prices down. Reach his technicians, reach his directors, reach his workers to sell your ideas. They will become excited about your ideas without worrying about whose budget is going to pay for it. They will squeeze their own buyer to buy from you and he will have to pay your price.

Working the market means teaching your sales executives how to negotiate as well as how to sell. They must know how to present price arguments as well as quality arguments.

Figure 1.1
What will the market bear? (an 11-step process)

Step 1
Allocate responsibility

Step 2
Set price policy objectives

Step 3
List decisions to be made

Step 4
Identify influencing factors

Step 5
Review market information

Step 6
Review competitive information

Step 7
Review cost data

Step 8
Establish strategy

Step 9
Set price

Step 10
Set cost and volume objectives

Step 11
Review price performance

WORK YOUR PROFITS

Look after the protection of your profit margins. For every low margin line, you need a high margin line to balance it. Don't go for a rigidly high unit price—because you will not sell enough volume. But don't go for volume at any price either. Work your product mix, be flexible with your pricing, use your price changes to their best advantage. Go for controlled but profitable growth. Keep the business tight, and keep your unit costs always under pressure.

DEVELOP YOUR COMPETITIVE EDGE

Make sure you offer something unique that your competitors do not offer. Promote this difference hard and make sure your customers want this special edge of yours. This will give you a firmer pricing base. When you must discount, then discount, but make sure that your discount policy is well controlled. Make sure you know why you are discounting. Be creative and put a time limit on all your discounts. Don't ever give money away for nothing—discounts must do something for you in exchange. Don't delegate discount decisions down the line to your salesman if you can avoid it. Get the best market information you can; verify it for truth.

Now you have read the instant version, why not go for the full course of home treatments? Read the rest of the book.

How Prices Affect Business Performance | 2

Before reading the chapter, complete the answers to these questions in the spaces on the left-hand side. Then without looking at the answers, read the chapter. Finally, complete the answers again, making any changes you think fit. Score both sets of your answers. This tells you how much the chapter has affected your opinion. Scores are at the end of the book (p. 193).

WOULD YOU MAKE IT AS A TOP BUSINESS MANAGER?

Q.1 *The Secretary of the Treasury is asking for your opinion about how manufacturing industry will respond if he enforces a rigid policy of price controls throughout the economy in an effort to contain inflation. What do you tell him?*
(Check the most appropriate column.)

	Very likely	Perhaps	Very unlikely
(a) *Product quality will be reduced*	✓		
(b) *Some product shortages will occur*	✓		
(c) *Inflation will be contained completely*			✓
(d) *Bankruptcies will increase*	✓		
(e) *Unemployment will increase*	✓		
(f) *The government will be popular*			✓

Score _____

_____

Before reading chapter.   *After reading chapter.*

Score _____

6

Q.2 *Whenever you study the management accounting figures of companies you plan to buy, you search for one kind of figure first. Which is it?*
(a) Growth in sales; (b) accounts receivable outstanding; (c) ratio of fixed cost to sales; (d) gross profit margin or contribution; (e) value added per employee?

d

Score _____

_____

Before reading chapter.   *After reading chapter.*

Score _____

5

Q.3 *You are in financial trouble. You sell a packaging service for drug companies; you take their pills and give them a coating of gelatin so that people can swallow them easily. Your machines are expensive. Your predecessor bought three new machines but you find you have sufficient work only for an extra one and a half machines. Although you are brand leader, you are working on very thin profit margins due to heavy competition. What action do you take?*

(a) Cut the price to compete with your rivals and to build new sales volume to fill up your three machines; (b) keep to your prices for your customers, but cut back on your other costs. Sell the three machines, get rid of the small customers and all those who are unprofitable; (c) hang on for a while to see how the market goes, but take savings in your overhead. Cut your sales force costs, reduce avertising. Give extended credit to see if this will help to hold customers; (d) sell two machines quickly. Hammer overhead costs such as administration and put extra money into the promotion budget; (e) search for a new acquisition or a new product?

d + e

Score   **Score**
_____

Before reading chapter.   After reading chapter.
                                                                              5
_____

Q.4 *Which pricing policy do you prefer, personally? There is no right or wrong answer, but the scores are allocated on the basis of the riskiness of the policy you prefer, and the difficulty of managing such a policy.*
(a) Never knowingly undersold—offering the lowest prices in the market; (b) offering the highest prices in the market; (c) some of your prices are low and you promote these heavily; (d) a price around the middle of the market, offering the same benefits as the market leaders; (e) a price above the main market, but offering some distinctive or unique aspect of quality or service.

d & c

Score   **Score**
_____

Before reading chapter.   After reading chapter.
                                                                              3
_____

Q.5 *As CEO, you are presented with four alternative strategies. Each of your VPs is arguing fiercely for his case. You have to make a decision. Which one?*

(a) The salespeople, backed by engineering, want a policy of fast growth. "If you don't invest, you'll die. If we put in three new machines, then we'll get the extra sales," runs their argument. (b) The controller wants to cut the costs of the business by reducing the advertising budget, and by taking other

overhead savings. He says that growth can be met cheaply through working extra overtime with existing resources. (c) The technical people want to push ahead with a radical new development which, if it comes off, could revolutionize the industry. If it fails, the business could be in trouble, but if it succeeds it could be a huge winner. (d) A rather dull plan is also available. It involves cutting back on costs here and there, plus some new investment in machinery, putting some funds in research and development, and controlling the business tightly all the time.

d

Score   **Score**
_____   _____

           Before reading chapter.   *After reading chapter.*   5
_____

Q.6   *There are established suppliers to a certain mature market. Which one of them would you prefer to be in order to make the most profit (total cash profit, not return on capital employed)?*

           (a) The brand leader with a 25% share of the market; (b) the number two or three brand with a 5% premium price over the average prices paid in the market; (c) the aggressive price cutter; (d) the specialized producer at the top end of the market?

A

Score   **Score**
_____   _____

           Before reading chapter.   *After reading chapter.*   5
_____

Scores

Above 25	Good result. You sound experienced.
19–24	Fair. Most people score here.
9–18	Perhaps you are not understanding the questions.
8 or less	You cannot be understanding the questions.

How Prices Affect Business Performance | 2

The city of Antwerp, throughout its history, has relied heavily for its supplies upon ships coming up the Scheldt estuary. The Duke of Parma, while he was besieging that city during the 16th century, found it impossible to blockade the estuary sufficiently so as to prevent food from reaching the noble citizen defenders. He fussed and fumed for a year in his attempt to starve the citizens.

He need not have worried, for the Antwerp city fathers did the job for him in the end, through their misguided pricing policy.

When supplies are short of any commodity which is in strong demand, then the price will go up. Such a law is fundamental, born of man's behavior, not of his legislation. The city fathers interfered with this natural law by bringing in a man-made rule which set upper limits on the price of food. Anyone in the city caught buying or selling food above the market price during the siege was punished, and severely.

The food merchants outside the city saw no profit in running the blockade of Spanish guns in order to achieve the ordinary kind of profits they could make daily in any country market. So they stopped supplying the city. The citizens meanwhile, no doubt pleased to find that food prices remained as stable as in normal times, saw no reason to conserve their demands, nor their appetites.

Ever since man started growing crops, and thereby found the means to stay in one place, he has needed markets. The prices of essential commodities have always been a matter of government interference. There are countless examples of government control over pricing activity which had perfectly laudable purposes but which, in the event, succeeded in producing the opposite effect from that which was intended.

The city fathers of Antwerp wanted to stop their hungry citizens being overcharged by merchants in a strong position. They wanted to ensure that food would be distributed to everyone in the city, not just to those with the money to pay for it. Thereby they hoped to maintain the conditions for a stable community that would be able to resist the attacks of the Spanish.

In the event, the city collapsed earlier than was necessary, much earlier. High prices for food would have conserved their food stocks. As it was, the food continued to be eaten as before. One day, almost without warning, the food ran out. The city surrendered within a week.

Question: *Did the word "twerp" originate with the Antwerp city fathers in the 16th century?*

In any organized market, prices obey certain laws of behavior. It is entirely possible for a government, a company or an individual trader to distort the market by following and obeying some theory of economics such as monetary policy, or a theory of marketing such as penetration pricing, or a practice of accountancy such as standard costing. If the chosen theory does not flow in harmony with the natural process of the market, the effects are always uncomfortable and often calamitous. The imposition of price control policies is nearly always very damaging to an economy.

Yet pricing is at the center of any government's economic policy—these days it is focused upon the control of inflation. Pricing policy is at the root of company philosophy. The average selling price of the material produced, when multiplied by the amount of material sold, produces the company revenue. When the costs of producing the material have been subtracted from this revenue, what remains is the future. The future could be bright with expansion possibilities, it could be clouded by bankruptcy, liquidation or forced sale. The future is dependent upon the equation of Prices times Volume of Sales minus Costs of all kinds.

If you were to examine 150,000 financial ratios from 240 different firms covering seven totally different industries, with the purpose of finding out what is the most important single factor leading to success in business management, you would come to one overwhelming conclusiom. You could look at the turnover of assets employed, the return on assets, growth; productivity of labor, control of inventory levels and control of debt levels; and you would conclude that all of those factors are important, together with many others. Some apply more strongly in manufacturing companies, while others are more important in service industries.

Yet over 90% of the variations of rate of return in all those companies, when measured consistently over three and a half years, could be traced to one single factor—the profit margin on sales. "No other single factor in our study had such a strong and consistent influence upon return on assets," reported Interfirm Comparison, the company that conducted the survey.

Companies place great emphasis upon their planning systems and control routines. Budgets, targets and policies are laid out for engineering, for production, for research and development. Marketing policy is debated in considerable detail. Finance, accounting and administration departments work according to their agreed plans. Purchasing, transport and distribution seek to improve their productivity. [All of those functions work efficiently because they each are handled by a specialist department with its specialist management.]

The management of pricing policy, however, is diffused at best and chaotic at worst in most companies. Very few companies have a Director of Pricing. As a result, pricing decisions are taken at different levels in the organization. Several departments contribute their point of view to the pricing decision. Management accounting, marketing, general management all want to be in-

Figure 2.1
Importance of price in overall marketing strategy

A consulting group carried out a study on how industry prices.* This study covered companies operating across a standard sample of industries, large companies and small.

We will quote results from this survey throughout this book. One basic question asked of all respondents was "How important to your company's marketing policy is your pricing strategy?" The table shows the answers.

Vital	17%	
Important	57%	*All*
Fairly important	25%	*respondents*
Not important	1%	
Vital	12%	*Those*
Important	53%	*selling*
Fairly important	34%	*capital*
Not important	1%	*goods*
Vital	20%	
Important	61%	*Components*
Fairly important	18%	
Not important	1%	
Vital	18%	
Important	58%	*Materials*
Fairly Important	21%	
Not important	3%	

Clearly, most companies in industry regard their pricing policy as being either vital or most important to their results. This is marginally more true of those supplying components to industry than those selling capital goods. Almost no company regards its pricing policy as being of no importance.

How British Industry Prices, Industrial Market Research, 1975.

volved in the process. Even the field salesman is often given the power to negotiate individual discounts with customers. The cumulative sum of the impact of all the decision-making influences upon the company's profit and growth performance is enormous.

Pricing policy needs special care and attention in a company, simply because so many different people influence it. The desire to head a company in the direction of all-out growth leads to a desire to knock down the price. The margins are tight, allowing little leeway for error. Any downturn in demand, however slight, can then be disastrous. At such a time, prices cannot be increased, so the pressure must be exerted upon costs. Services are stripped to the bone. The quality of the material deteriorates. The quality of the company's operation is reduced in every direction.

> Question for undischarged bankrupts: *Did you say you were going all out for sales volume at any price?*

A cut-price policy often leads to doom, as it did in the case of the Rolls Royce aircraft engine, unless the business is carefully controlled. The company went bankrupt after it tried to capitalize its research and development costs in order to shore up its profits, and was rescued by the government of the day. Cut-price automobile insurance was doomed—the business was poorly controlled and became a runaway monster. Certain travel agents were doomed when inflation in Spain drove up their costs after they had sold, and been paid for, vacations at cut prices. Now travel agents have surcharge clauses—particularly for fuel price increases or exchange rate fluctuations.

Some companies can do very well at cut prices, but they have to be razor efficient to do it; they must work their resources very hard; they hammer their overheads to the bone. For the price cutters, the line between success and failure is extremely thin. Supermarkets start making their net profits each week at 4:30 on a Saturday afternoon. Laker Airways could run a cut-price airline while it was very small, and while it had low overhead. While it was small, the large rivals did not copy it. But when Laker went after a major share of the transatlantic routes and was joined in doing so by another small rival, Air Florida, then the giants had to follow. Laker crashed. British Airways sustained huge losses and so did Pan Am. With very large fixed costs, and because of the recession in air travel and enough spare aircraft lying idle on the ground to equip Laker Airways completely, British Airways suffered from its policy of matching low cost operators from its corporate base of high fixed cost. Trying to sustain 18% of the intercontinental air travel market with the national flag carrier of a country with less than 2% of the world's population is courting disaster, if your pricing policy means that you must carry people to New York at a cost of 2¢ a mile! The chairman of BOAC, the original international part of British Airways, knew how to get his organization to make money regularly. He sold at sensible prices, and he always kept his management team at least one airplane short. So they made their existing planes work that little bit harder. That is how to make money.

Figure 2.2
Why do companies fail?

In 1975, bankruptcies in Britain hit an all-time high after the 1974 recession. One of the world's leading accounting companies made a study of these failures and listed the principal conclusions.[2]

COMPANY FAILURES: THE SIGNS

Organization	An inflexible management structure.
	A slow response to change.
	Accounting information poor.
Controls	Deficient budgetary control.
	Deficient cash flow plan.
	Deficient costing system.
Balance sheet	Over-trading.
	Over-leveraging.
	Over-commitment.

COMPANY FAILURE: THE PROCESS

One	Management is accident-prone.
	Management is sluggish.
Two	Deterioration of financial position.
	"Creative accounting."
	Deterioration of customer service.
	Postponed maintenance.
Three	Desperate search for capital at any price.

THREAT AVOIDANCE

Set challenging targets for profits or margins, as well as challenging sales or market share totals.

The conclusion was seen to be inescapable. Companies must set themselves challenging targets for profits and margins. And that leads directly to pricing policy.

IQ test: (a) *Which pairs of words go together—cheap, select, nasty, expensive?*

Or, in the airline business, you can do it another way. You can lift the quality of service; you can demonstrate your reliability and timekeeping; you can provide personal attention—if you keep it small and tight like Swissair. They do a little price cutting, here and there, but it is always kept out of the Swiss market. They sell the occasional cut-price flight to Johannesburg via Swissair, but only in London or in Amsterdam, never in Zurich. And in this way, their airline is profitable and their customers like them and compare them favorably with other airlines. They will never be the biggest in the world. But they will be one of the happiest. Who wants to be the biggest, if you have to keep creeping to your government every year for a hand-out or to roll over your loans, or to pinch and scrape every aspect of service and cost so that your customers and staff are not too pleased? Because that's what being a cut-price operator means.

IQ test: (b) *Which of the foregoing pairs of words would you prefer as the image for your business?*

HOW TO DOUBLE YOUR PROFITS

Here are three ways in which you might double your profits. We will make some assumptions to start with; then you can put in the real figures for your own company.

Let us make the assumption that you are the chief executive of the meat products division of a multinational food company. Your products are delivered fresh daily in trucks to shops, restaurants and hotels. Your meat loaves are of excellent quality, using top class pork with a high meat content. You have just installed a new traveling oven, the cost of which would frighten you if you thought about it too much. You also have a cold storage, first-class butchers (you can lose a lot of money here if the butchers are not efficient), and twenty people on the packing line. Your sales are $10,000,000 a year. Your annual gross profit after deducting your $6,000,000 of direct costs of materials, and the labor involved in production, is $4,000,000. Your overhead, including transportation and sales costs, is $3,500,000. This leaves you with a net profit of $500,000. That, incidentally, is a perfectly reasonable, although not exciting, net profit in this kind of industry. It gives you a return on assets of about 20%, because your capital is valued at $2,500,000.

Now suppose you want to double this profit of $500,000. Let us say that you find some means of doing it through increasing the sales volume. Perhaps you are planning to develop a super range of new products. Assume for the moment that the same selling price holds as before, and that you can also squeeze the extra production from your traveling oven, and that you can find space in your cold storage for the extra volume. Furthermore, you can also find space in your vehicles to carry the new products to the market. Additionally, all the new products will be sold to existing customers without taking sales away from your present range of products. (The assumptions become increasingly unlikely.)

Figure 2.3
Three ways to double your profits

In this business	($000)				
Sales revenue	$10		(a) If you increase the sales by 25% and hold your fixed costs steady	$12.5	
Direct costs, materials, production, labor	$6	$4 materials $2 labor			
				$7.5	
Fixed costs, overhead, distribution, sales	$3.5			$3.5	
Net profit	$0.5		**you double the profits**	$1	

(b) Hold your sales steady	$10		(c) Increase your average prices by 5% (through a different product sales mix) holding sales volume level and all costs level	$10.5	
and lower your material costs by 12½%	$3.5	materials		$4	
	$2	labor		$2	
holding your fixed costs steady	$3.5			$3.5	
you will double your profits	$1		**you will double your profits**	$1	

You would have to increase your sales volume by no less than 25% in order to double your profits. And you would have to obtain that sales increase without incurring any extra cost to yourself at all, except in the amount of materials you buy. You are not allowed to increase the size of your sales force.

Supposing you wanted to double your profits another way. This time on the original basis of costs, you plan to cut down your cost of production. Well, you are stuck with your traveling oven, now that you have it. And you cannot easily reduce the size of your cold storage. If you want to maintain your present level of sales, then you will have to go on calling on your existing customers using the same vehicles and men as you have at present.

You will have to take the savings in your direct production costs. But can you reduce the amount of meat you use, or reduce the number of butchers you employ or the number of people on your packing line? That would be very difficult, unless they have not been used efficiently up to now. You might replace them by some mechanized means, but in that case, you would have to add extra cost in the form of new equipment.

No, the savings will have to come from buying cheaper materials, or in developing some new recipe whereby the meat can be mixed with soya flour or some other similar excuse for quality that is always used by companies who cannot get their pricing strategy right.

Your meat and other materials cost you $4,000,000 a year. So to double your profits you are going to have to develop a new recipe or find a new source of supply that will produce the same quality of meat and materials for you, but at a cost of $3,500,000 instead of $4,000,000. Then you will have saved 12½% of your material costs, and provided you do not lose any sales you will have doubled your profits.

There is a sting in that proviso, *provided you don't lose any sales*. Do you really think that you can degrade your product quality by one-eighth and your customers will not notice the difference? They will and your sales will fall. And if they don't fall, then you have been over-engineering your products—making them too good for the market. (Many companies do exactly this without knowing it.)

Of course, it may be entirely possible for you to reduce the costs of production by one-eighth, just as it may be entirely possible for you to double your profits by increasing your sales volume by one-fourth. But how much simpler to re-organize your marketing policy a little here and there. Upgrade a few products here, develop sales to quality-conscious customers there, mix up your selling prices with promotional discounts, and teach your salesmen how to negotiate prices efficiently with the biggest buyers. You can double your profits if you can obtain an average price increase of only 5%. If you can change your product mix to improve your overall margin by 5%, then you will have doubled your profits.

The conclusion of the Interfirm Comparison study already mentioned is inescapable. Only one single factor, profit margin on sales, had such a strong and consistent influence upon the return on assets of the 240 companies in the study over the years.

Incidentally, the study also concluded that the second most important factor appeared to be the tight control of overhead of all kinds. That was found to be more important than growth.

Growth is an important factor in profitability, but the cost of getting the growth may be exorbitant. To find a success, many failures may have to be experienced. The cost of development may be too high a drain on the company's profits. Or the cost of entry into a new market may be too high.

The alternative route to growth, that of cutting prices solely in an attempt to achieve it, is not an alternative at all. It usually leads to disaster, because the profit margins which are supposed to be fattened by the growth are themselves reduced directly by the price reductions.

The penalty for not getting the pricing right is very high. One year, a major and efficient company in the switchgear industry based its pricing policy on the fact that between seven and nine large generator sets worth $90,000,000 would be ordered by a large public utility. They priced them upon the basis of full costs plus profit—very sensibly. Then they went looking for overseas orders for their generating sets which would be sold at very low cost. The accountants in the company argued, as accountants will, that the full overhead would be recovered by the sales of the domestic sets, and therefore the company could afford to price the overseas sets low. That suited the company salesmen, who argued, as salesmen will, that the price would have to be very low to compete overseas.

The price offered overseas was low enough to win the orders, sure enough. Unfortunately, the orders for the original full cost sets, upon which the company's fortunes for that year depended, did not materialize. The losses ran into millions.

PRICING AND POWER: THE PARADOX

Prices are a function of power. If your demand is strong, you are free to move upward on price. If your profits are good, you are free to move downward on price, because you can afford it. You have power because options are available to you.

If your demand is weak, you cannot afford to move your price upward.

If, at the same time, your profits are poor—perhaps because of the fact that your demand is weak—then you are powerless. Move your prices upward and your competitors steal your business. Move your prices down and the risk of increasing your losses is very great.

It pays to be profitable in a market where demand is strong.

During a recent recession two of the world's top managers were puzzling over an identical problem. One, in Copenhagen, was sitting on top of too much inventory of his product. Demand was reasonably strong but weakening a little. The costs of the interest charges on the excess inventory were worrying him. And he wanted to liven up the market a bit. So, as boss of the Danish Bacon Corporation—a profitable organization—he decided to make an aggressive move in the world market. He cut the price by $100 a ton wholesale, about 3% or so. This caused the other producers a problem. The chief executive of

Figure 2.4
Five Pricing Strategies

Objective	Strategy	When generally used	Procedure	Advantages	Disadvantages
High short-term profit	**Top of Market** Market skimming at high prices.	No comparable competitive products. New product innovation. Little danger of competitor entry due to patent control, high R & D costs, high promotion costs, or raw material control. Uncertain costs. Short life-cycle. Inelastic demand. High risk to buyer in the use of the product.	Determine preliminary customer reaction. Charge premium price for product distinctiveness in short run. Early buyers will pay more because of higher present value to them. Then, gradually reduce price to tap successive market levels.	Protects against adverse cost variances. Requires smaller investment. Provides funds quickly to cover development costs Limits demand until production is expanded. Suggests higher value in buyer's mind. Emphasizes value rather than cost as a guide to pricing.	Assumes that a market exists at high price. May result in management complacency. Attracts competition. Likely to underestimate ability of competitors to copy product. Discourages some buyers from trying the product (connotes high profits).

To obtain a reasonable volume at a higher than average price.	**Upmarket** Slide-down demand curve(version of skimming, without sacrificing long-term objectives).	By established companies launching innovations. Durable goods Medium life span.	Taps successive layers of demand at highest prices possible. Then deliberately drops the price leading the market. Rate of price change is slow enough to add significant volume at each successive price level, but fast enough to prevent large competitor from becoming established on a low-cost volume basis.	Emphasizes value rather than cost as a guide to pricing. Provides rapid return on investment. Provides slight cushion against adverse cost variances. Provides sound trading base. Basis for becoming price leader.	Requires broad knowledge of competitive product developments. Requires much documented experience. Discourages some buyers from buying at initial high price. Requires market experience.

Figure 2.4 (continued)
Five pricing strategies

Objective	Strategy	When generally used	Procedure	Advantages	Disadvantages
To tap primary demand	**Competitive** Competitive at the market price.	Several comparable products. Growing market. Medium to long product life span. Known costs.	Start with final price and work back to cost. Use customer surveys and studies of competitors' prices to approximate final price; deduct selling margins; adjust product and production and selling methods to sell at this price and still make necessary profit margins.	Meets buyers' expectations of price. Known market situation.	Leads to a "me-too" product policy. Limited flexibility. Limited room for error. Slower recovery of investment. Must rely on product difference.

	Downmarket				
Stimulate market growth and capture and hold a satisfactory market share at a profit through low prices. Become strongly entrenched to generate profits over a long period.	Market penetration.	Long product life span. Mass market. Easy market entry. Demand is highly sensitive to price. Unit costs of production and distribution decrease rapidly as quantity of output increases. Product with no distinction. No specialist market willing to pay premium for newest and best. Customers taking quality for granted.	Charge low prices to create a mass market resulting in cost advantages derived from larger volume. Look at lower end of demand curve to set price low enough to attract a large customer base. Also review past and competitor prices.	Discourages actual and potential competitor inroads because of apparent low profit margins. Emphasizes cost more than value in pricing. Allows maximum exposure and penetration in minimum time. May maximize long-term profits if competition is minimized.	Assumes volume is always responsive to price reductions, which isn't always true. Relies on low price to stimulate demand which doesn't always work. May create more business than production capacity available. Requires significant investment. Small errors often result in large losses.

Figure 2.4 (continued)
Five Pricing Strategies

Objective	Strategy	When generally used	Procedure	Advantages	Disadvantages
Keep competitors out of market or eliminate existing ones.	**Bottom End** Floor price.	Used more often in consumer markets or with low-risk industrial materials for low cost producers. Manufacturers may use this approach on one or two products, with other prices meeting, or higher than, those of competitors. When overhead is thin and profit is obtained from selected big deals at razor thin margins.	Price at low levels so that market is unattractive to possible competitors. Set price as close as possible to total unit cost. As increased volume allows lower cost, pass advantage to buyers via lower prices. If costs decline rapidly with increases in volume, can start price below cost.	Discourages potential competitors because of apparent low profit margins. Limits competitive activity and expensive requirements to meet them. May be useful for utilizing spare capacity outside normal markets.	Must offer reduced services which permit lower price (limited credit, delivery, or promotions). Long-term payback period. Needs very tight cost control. Risk of substantial losses.

the competitor in the US market refused to follow the Danes' price cut. He judged it would lead to a price war—one he could not stand because he had just spent a huge amount on new equipment and his company's profits were wafer-thin. The Danes increased their share of the market because they could afford the price cut out of their profits.

At the same time, a top manager responsible for huge oil refining operations in the UK found that the world glut of oil, caused by very weak demand, was causing him big losses. Gasoline prices are fiercely competitive at the pumps and price wars between local dealers often rage. But the oil producers' prices tend to follow each other in reasonable line together. Three months previously, most oil companies had put up their prices by about 10¢ a gallon, but offered their dealers promotional discount "support" to ease them through the price increases. Later they withdrew this "support." But the full price failed to stick, and they restored the dealer support because the market was so weak.

So they all had another go at increasing their prices. On the average, most companies needed a price increase of 12¢ a gallon in order to break even on their refining costs. But their new high prices fell short of that. They could get no more without closing off demand further.

The manager in Copenhagen could afford to cut his prices because his company was profitable. He put his competitors under severe pressure because their profitability was stretched tight at the time, and they could not afford to follow the price cut.

On the other hand, the oil companies could not afford to put up their prices. Market demand was so weak, while the supply side was in glut, that there was no way for them to recover their profits in the short term. The seesaws of the oil industry will continue through the years ahead. Glut and shortage follow each other persistently in the oil industry. Most years the oil companies win; some years they lose.

The market and the competition are the key determining factors in price. If the market will not pay the price, then its suppliers will continue to suffer losses—until their costs of production come down.

The paradox in the story is that two managers facing the same problem decided to take opposite courses of action. One cut his price, while the other tried to increase it. Which action they were able to take depended upon the market demand, the competition and their profits.

SUMMARY

Most companies pay a great deal of attention to providing efficient manufacturing, sound products, good customer service, and excellent cost and accounting controls. Yet fundamental to their business is the question of overall profit margin on sales. And pricing policy is at the heart of the profit margin. In business, there are many VPs of Sales and many VPs of Production. There are few VPs of Pricing.

Few people have the necessary training or experience to handle all the complexities of pricing decisions in a company. Even fewer have access to the full range of information they need to make a pricing decision—particularly information about the market. Yet pricing decisions are dispersed in a multitude of ways throughout the organization and at many levels.

Pricing decisions are often made arbitrarily. They are often based upon firm estimates of costs but very uncertain estimates of the market. They are interfered with by managers down the line offering concessions and discounts, particularly for big customers. So pricing practice becomes distorted. Pricing decisions are often rushed. Where many pricing decisions have to be made constantly by managers in different parts of the business, a standard formula is used. As a result, the pricing system becomes inflexible and cost-related, when what is wanted is a system that allows pricing to be flexible and market-related.

Pricing decisions can lead to disaster, particularly when they are based upon the simple notion that if the prices were much lower, then people would buy much more. This simple law of economics works reasonably well where large numbers are concerned, with broad markets and undifferentiated products, such as commodities.

> Tip for investors. *When your company decides to "pile it high and sell it cheap,"
> then invest in* Dow Jones. *Their paper,* The Wall Street Journal, *carries the
> best executive job advertisements.*

But within the microeconomics of the individual business enterprise that general trend is swamped by distortions. Different product qualities will distort the trend, so will advertising and sales pressure, so will the channel of trade through which the product must be sold. Further distortions will occur if the market is segmented into some buyers with a very strong need for the product and others with a weak preference.

Pricing policy has a marked and direct impact upon profitability. More so even than sales volume or cost cutting—at least in the short term.

*   *   *

Now go back to the questionnaire at the start of this chapter and complete it again.

A Business Planning Process Based | 3
upon the Market

Before reading the chapter, complete the answers to these questions in the spaces on the left-hand side. Then without looking at the answers, read the chapter. Finally, complete the answers again, making any changes you think fit. Score both sets of your answers. This tells you how much the chapter has affected your opinion. Scores are at the end of the book (p. 194).

PRICING QUESTIONS THAT MAKE FINANCIAL OFFICERS UNEASY

Q.1   *A study shows that 81% of industrial companies use costs plus a margin of profit to calculate their selling prices. 15% of them also report that they rarely, if ever, modify the selling price they obtain in this way. In an ideal world, how would you set about pricing your goods, assuming you could get all the information you want?*

(a) Calculate your costs, add on a margin and thus set your selling price;
(b) study the market, determine your selling price and then set cost objectives;
(c) copy the competitors' prices and provide cost budgets; (d) ask the sales force for their opinion; (e) ask your accountant?

Score   **Score**

_____   _____

Before reading chapter.   *After reading chapter.* 5   *b*

_____

Q.2   *You own an old country-town hotel with oil heating. In 1972 your fuel bill was $2,500. In 1985 it is expected to be $20,000. You cannot believe it; the figures are crippling your business. Why has this state of affairs come about; what is the principal reason?*

(a) The formation of a cartel among oil producers (OPEC); (b) the extremely high cost of getting oil from new sources; (c) an overwhelming increase in demand for oil; (d) oil companies' profits and government taxes; (e) gradually increasing demand faced with gradually shortening supply.

Score   **Score**

_____   _____

Before reading chapter.   *After reading chapter.* 5   *e.*

_____

Q.3   *A friend of yours has a son who was a brilliant amateur light heavyweight boxer. Now he has turned professional and his father is acting as his manager. Your friend has received a wire from a Las Vegas promoter asking him how much he wants to fight the world's number two light heavyweight. He wants to take the fight but does not know how much to ask. What advice do you give him?*

(a) Ask for his travel and hotel expenses plus enough money to assure the boy a living wage until his next fight; (b) suggest he try for $500,000 to see what they say; (c) do it for expenses only because the publicity will be good and you can all take a vacation while you are there; (d) ask another couple of managers of champion boxers for their view of the market; (e) ask the promoter to make you an offer.

Score   **Score**
_____

Before reading chapter.   *After reading chapter.*   5   d
_____

Q.4   *Here are five objectives in a business planning process; put them in order of sequence, first to last.*

	No.		
(a)	___	*Establish your objective in terms of market share*	___
(b)	___	*Establish your profit objectives*	___
(c)	___	*Set your pricing objectives*	___
(d)	___	*Establish unit cost of production objectives*	___
(e)	___	*Develop your manufacturing plan objectives*	

Score   **Score**
_____

Before reading chapter.   *After reading chapter.*
_____

Q.5   *Gold is a virtually useless metal. As with other non-renewable resources it is dwindling in supply—the U.S.S.R. and South Africa are the two principal sources. Its industrial applications can mostly be substituted by cheaper products. In two years, the price of gold has fallen from $800 an ounce to less than $400 an ounce. Would you invest in gold for the long run?*

(a) Yes, with enthusiasm, a proportion of your funds; (b) no, too risky even for the long term; (c) you can't say; (d) put in all your savings.

Score   **Score**
_____

Before reading chapter.   *After reading chapter.*   ?   C
_____

Q.6   *The hens on your farm can be fed in such a way that they will produce eggs with white shells. Or, by using a different diet, they will produce eggs with brown shells. In either case, the costs of feed, the yield and conversion are identical. It is as cheap to produce white eggs as to produce brown eggs.*

What would you do if you were an egg farmer selling eggs at a roadside produce stand?

(a) Produce an equal mixture of brown and white eggs to offer the market a choice at identical prices; (b) produce all-white eggs or all-brown eggs, it does not matter which, but minimize your costs by not splitting the diet; (c) buy whatever feed is cheapest at the time and let the egg color look after itself; (d) find out what the market prefers and then deliberately produce that color; (e) produce two colors but deliberately price the color the market prefers higher than the other color?

Score   **Score**
_____   _____

            Before reading chapter.   *After reading chapter.*   5   d
_____   _____

Scores

Above 27	Very good.
21–26	Most experienced executives score here.
15–20	You *know* you can do better.
Up to 15	Oops!

A Business Planning Process | 3
Based upon the Market

The flight path to Jan Smuts airport takes you over the old gold fields of Johannesburg, worked out and exhausted in the 1930s. American and other goldfield owners moved them to more profitable, deeper mines elsewhere. They left behind them the waste earth in the form of slurry tips which the local authorities grassed over for use as parks and playing fields. Fifty years later, the tips still would be recognizable as such to anyone used to the slurry tips of coal mines, such as those, for example, in South Wales.

In 1972, the gold price was $35 an ounce and soccer matches were being played on the tops of the old gold mines. But then we all lurched a little toward economic anarchy. The ravages of inflation swept around the world, followed by recession. In tandem with those two, as always, was a deeply felt unease about currency. The pattern of human behavior was predictable. During economic disturbance, people leave money alone if they can, and take to gold. Since time immemorial people have behaved thus whenever they doubted currency. This happened in the 1970s despite the fact that governments around the world have tried to take their economies away from gold.

Observation: *The people often have more sense than the governments they elect.*

And so, as night follows day, the price of gold increased. From an "official" price of $35, gold began to be traded freely at $100 an ounce. Soon the Standard Bank of South Africa was selling the one-ounce Krugerrand coin over the counter. It had a nominal face value of 80¢ or so but an actual price of $300. But then it was 1974, the coin was made of pure gold, the demand was strong and people were willing to pay the price. "Tuck a couple in the heel of your shoe," said a leading South African stockbroker to me. "When you get them home, they'll be worth more than that." And he was right.

If the market demand is strong and supply is short, the price will go up. The costs of production have got nothing to do with this logic. If the supply increases but the demand remains strong, prices will reduce slightly as buyers seek to play off one supplier against another. But if the demand weakens, or if people are penniless or otherwise short of money, prices will collapse. Often, for short periods of time, prices will collapse below the cost of production. Suppliers find this to be a very uncomfortable situation; carried on to excess, it leads to the extinction of the business enterprise.

26

Few people would argue with this idea, which is so easily demonstrable. But what does business do, in practice?

In the face of this logic, it seems unbelievable, but business actually tries hard to set selling prices that for the most part are based upon their costs of production. Take this book, for example. The cost of the typesetting has been calculated. So has the cost of printing a certain number of copies, together with other direct costs of production. An estimate has been made of the total overhead costs of running the business, which are then divided by the total number of book sales expected in the chosen period.

That gives you the "overhead recovery," usually expressed in the form of a percentage margin on sales. That margin allows for sales and publicity costs, and the selling price must also allow for some sort of percentage margin to the book trade. A system of standard costing such as this is used to set the selling price of goods. Admittedly, when the calculations have been made, the "market price" idea enters into the calculations. If the standard cost calculations have resulted in too high a selling price and not enough profit, then the calculations are juggled to make them fit. If the standard cost results in too low a selling price, then a little more will be added to the "quality" in some way. Cost may be added in binding, for example.

With this book, what really matters is the market and the competitive price of similar publications. What will the trade think of a book priced in odd fractions? In that case the figures would be rounded off to just below a "price point." What would buyers think of a book that is excessively high in price? What is meant by "excessively"? Suppose the book were priced too cheaply; wouldn't that put some buyers off, thinking it to be of poor value? To answer that question we need judgment, based upon experience of the market. Costs hardly enter into it. The truth is that there are hundreds of ways to calculate prices by using cost accounting systems. But no one in the world has yet developed an adequate means of measuring universally what the market will bear. That has always been based upon guesswork, backed by experience.

Pricing remains an art. In a few narrow markets—where demand is stable, where supply is stable, where pricing history is well documented, where service differences are negligible and where the products are undifferentiated—the demand at various prices can be fairly well calculated. Mostly, we live in an unstable supply/demand situation.

We deliberately set out to distort the process of the market in our favor by marketing or advertising more effectively than our competitor. We cannot easily predict what extra premium can be demanded from the market for that factor.

When you next fly to Johannesburg, take a window seat. See the excavating equipment working on the old goldfield slurry tips. They are screening all the old earth they once threw away as useless in order to extract whatever gold they can find. It is a very expensive process. But it pays them to do it, because today the price of gold is around $400 an ounce. A little while ago, the gold price touched no less than $800 an ounce.

Figure 3.1
Pricing methods used in industry

Principal method described

Cost-related systems   ══════════════════ 81%

Either adding a fixed percentage to cost or taking a fixed margin off
selling price.

Non-cost-related systems ═══ 19%

The survey shows little difference between suppliers of components,
capital goods and material suppliers.

*EXTENT TO WHICH SELLING PRICES BASED PRIMARILY
UPON COST ARE MODIFIED BY NON-COST-RELATED
FACTORS.*

Usually   ═══ 21%
Frequently   ═══ 19%
Sometimes   ══════ 45%
Rarely   ══ 15%

Suppliers of capital goods are slightly more disposed to modify their
prices based upon some other noncost factor.
These summary results show an appalling situation. Four-fifths of the
surveyed companies selling products to industry used cost-related
systems to set selling prices. (The same was revealed in surveys taken in
the United States, the United Kingdom and elsewhere.) More than half
of the companies altered prices only "sometimes" or "rarely." A very
substantial proportion of industrial companies are still living in the dark
ages of the industrial revolution, when all you had to do was to
produce the product and the world would demand it.

Source: *How British Industry Prices*, Industrial Market Research, 1975.

Gold prices have not gone up because the cost of getting the gold out of the
ground has gone up (although it has, of course). Anglo American has opened
up the old slurry tips again because the price is so high that it pays them to do
so, and it still leaves them with a profit.
And that is the proper role of costs. The critical pricing decisions in business
need to be based upon an idea of what the market will bear. What volume is

likely to be sold at what level of price? What level of quality must we produce in order to compete with others at that price? Finally, how do we produce at that cost and still leave ourselves a profit? That is the correct sequence for decision-making and is in accordance with the natural laws of economic and human behavior.

You may argue, from your experience of how your own company works, that the situation cannot be so bad. Surely all companies take notice of the market place and of their competition? Surely a large number of companies use market-related information to calculate their selling price?

Most companies use the cost-plus method as a basis for their pricing policy. Some of those companies, it is true, modify their selling price according to the market situation. But many more rarely or only sometimes modify their cost-plus price because of competition or because of the market.

MARKET-RELATED PRICING. NINE STEPS IN ESTABLISHING A BUSINESS PLAN

To develop any business plan sensibly, you must start by looking at the market to see if it gives you any room for entry and, if so, under what conditions. You may examine first the secondary sources of information about the market—the published data, the information which exists already and is freely available to those who want to dig it out. The fact that that is a most neglected area of marketing does not make it any less important. The author has found that the cheapest and quickest way of avoiding errors in marketing is to explore that area thoroughly. Then conduct primary market research of your own on the key factors related to your idea.

Now compare what you plan to offer the market with what the competition offers. Describe your offering's strengths and weaknesses against the leading product in the market, and also against the product which comes closest to yours in character. Describe also the differences between the applications offered by your product compared to those of the competition, and remember also to compare your service against that of the competition. Look for what the market wants and see how far you meet that requirement compared to the competition. Ask yourself, can any distinction be built into your product which the competition does not have? It is vital to build in unique product differences, because this is what will later enable you to obtain your price and to hold off the competition. Search for tangible differences if you can, unique properties that customers can see for themselves or touch or that you can demonstrate easily.

Calculate the sizes of the different segments of the market, those clusters of demand that share similar characteristics and that make up the various sub-markets. How are those segments made up in terms of sales volume and revenue? Such calculations are often difficult to make because data are not readily available, so a determined effort toward thoroughness will pay handsome dividends.

Where will your product idea fit into the segments? Calculate your objectives in terms of market share extended over a period of time, perhaps three to five

Figure 3.2
What are the non-cost-related systems which two companies use?

Use general level
of competitors' prices   59%

Investigation of
customer reaction   21%

Consult sales force   9%

Follow market leader   8%

Other system (e.g., trial
and error)   3%

Even those companies which principally use non-cost-related factors to determine their selling prices referred to competitors' prices more than they conducted market studies to determine their prices. At least that is an improvement on using simple cost-plus. All of these companies calculate their costs but they do not let them rule their decisions. If the costs come out too high to enable them to make a profit, they either find a way of reducing their costs or they do not go ahead with the product.

Consulting the sales force is a certain way to drive down your selling prices toward the floor. Unless it is handled with great skill and the sales force is objective, it will be the worst method of all.

A further check on these issues was taken in the survey by asking companies whether they ever investigated the acceptability of their selling prices among customers before finally fixing their prices. Some 66% said they did not.

years ahead. Calculate also the effect of your entry upon the existing competition. If you are successful, they will not stay idle—they will counterattack, they will defend the important sectors of their business, and they will copy your approach. You may need to design a second generation of your product to replace the original and to meet competitors' action.

Now you can turn the objectives into a sales forecast that determines the company's budget. The forecast will include an estimate of the selling price after discounts, and the detailed unit volume that will be required from manufacturing.

Figure 3.3
The business plan based upon market-related prices

How much will the market bear?	Examine market	Primary research – secondary research
	Compare product to competition	Features – services – applications
	Calculate size of market segments	Revenue – volume – seasonality
	Calculate market share objective	Revenue – volume – seasonality
	Calculate sales forecast	Price – revenue – units – discounts
Objectives and plans	Set profit objectives	Total money – ratio to sales – ratio to capital employed
	Develop plans to achieve goals	Marketing – sales – distribution – promotion – finance – administration
How little must it cost?	Establish cost objectives	Direct costs – semidirect – overhead
	Design manufacturing plan	Unit volume – unit cost – inventory levels – timetable

---

All the other departmental plans in the business can now be devised, followed by the detailed manufacturing and distribution cost objectives for the product.

It is now the task of engineering, of research and of development to work within those cost objectives in order to produce the product. They may say the cost objectives are impossible to meet. They usually do say so, as a matter of fact. So there will be constant review of objectives and plans until a fit can be established between what is desirable and what is possible. This is always an annoying stage involving a considerable amount of debate and frequent friction. Whereas compromise is probably required by everyone, what should not be compromised is the essential and original calculation of the volume to be obtained at a certain unit price. Since that was the best guess at the time, it will remain so throughout. But there will be a great temptation to fudge the number later, when cost targets are found to be impossible to meet. There will be pressure

---

Figure 3.4
Competition factors

Four questions to ask about competition.

How will competition react to your price? Is there a past pattern of reaction?

What is the basic price behavior of competition?

What is the availability (actual or potential) of competing and substitute products? How similar? How quick to react to your actions?

Have your competitors' pricing strategies significantly affected your sales volume?

Ten questions to ask about customers.

Does the product fill a real need or requirement? How many customers need the product?

How much are customers willing to pay?

How much can they pay?

What quantities of the product do customers need?

What is the saving to buyer (return-on-investment or cost saving)?

What is the degree of price sensitivity (impact of price on sales volume)?

What are the buying habits and motives?

Do customers shop around for your type of product (make price comparisons)?

What is the degree of price awareness?

---

to raise the calculated selling price and to keep to the estimate for the volume of sales simply in order to produce the necessary profit. The logic of this is absurd, of course.

Note: *That process is called "moving the target toward the arrow."*

After agreement between the parties involved, the detailed manufacturing plan can be designed. The plan must be followed by the usual reviews of performance according to plan and the necessary adjustments in the light of results. At those subsequent stages, the price itself will need adjustment. At that time, the company is sensitized to the market demand, and the market itself takes over the primary influence upon the business.

This, you may say, is all very well in theory, but how would it work out in practice? Let us suppose that your neighbor's wife has announced her intention to make quilts, tablecloths and other such items sewn beautifully in exquisite patchwork designs.

Her family finances the purchase of some material from a fabric shop sufficient for making one quilt, let us say. She spends several hours in the living room cutting this material into squares and sewing them together. She stuffs it. Then she takes it, folded nicely into a linen bag, to a shop that sells fabrics. The shop belongs to a big chain and the manager explains that she will have to go to the main office. She is learning the hard way the traumas of being a saleswoman.

A little shop selling gifts is her next call. The owner likes the quilt. "How much is it?" she is asked. Having all her costs at her fingertips, she has calculated that she could run off several each week at about $5.00 an hour for labor, plus material, plus a little more for profit. She tells the shop owner the price. "Oh, that's too much," says the owner, and your neighbor's wife begins to learn more of the traumas of selling, because all buyers always think that things cost too much. She pares her price down and the store owner agrees to buy the quilt and orders a couple more.

Within two months your neighbor's wife is inundated with orders. She cannot get help because no one is willing to work for only $5.00 an hour. The financing costs have leapt, particularly since the shop seems to take a long time to pay their bills. This time it is your neighbor's family that is being reminded of one of the other traumas of salesmanship. The sale is never made until the money is in the bank.

Within three months your neighbor's wife collapses with exhaustion and spends all the revenue from the patchwork quilt enterprise on convalescence in Bermuda.

That is the wrong way to do it.

Now let us assume that at this stage your own wife decides to take a hand and help her neighbor's enterprise. She wants to get it restarted on a sound commercial basis. Your wife searches out the shops that would most likely stock patchwork items. She notes first what sells and at what price and where. She talks to the shopkeepers. She creates some original ideas to make something different from the existing products.

Then she works out a budget showing what money might be earned from different items sold in varying quantities. She has a look at some competitors' products, studies a little of their company background. How do they make things, how do they sell them, are they profitable? She develops some special ideas of her own based upon what the competitors are *not* offering. She has an idea of the price at which she will sell her chosen items. She will need, then, a production plan that will show her how long she and her neighbor can afford to spend in making each item, and how much she can afford to spend on material. Is there a way to save money on material? Could she use a blend of cheap and expensive materials? That would keep down her unit costs and allow a profit margin at the price she has chosen. Now she can make her production plan.

This, you may say, is no different in reality from the process of marketing and, of course, it is almost identical. It does seem incredible that so many companies conduct their enterprises as in the first example of the neighbor's wife, using a product-oriented approach. And they modify it only occasionally.

The business planning process does put price at the front of the calculation, however, and it also puts at the front the company's profit objective. From those two calculations, added to a forecast of sales volume, the entire operation can now be programed.

Incidentally, if, when you go to South Africa, a stockbroker tells you to put a couple of Krugerrand in the heel of your shoe because the price will go up, you should do what he says. If you take all the known reserves of gold in the world and multiply them by five, assuming that we find five times more in the future than we know exists today—a very unlikely assumption—then we will only have sufficient gold to last the increase in demand for another 21 years.

So what will happen to the gold price then?

SUMMARY

As the world slowly becomes short of nonrenewable material resources, if the demand for these resources continues inexorably on the increase, prices will go up. There is no force which can stop them in the long run.

So producers will turn to the most unlikely and expensive sources for their supplies, such as discovering new sources of oil 500 fathoms beneath the North Sea, followed by drilling through ancient volcanic rock or dragging the shale beaches of Venezuela. If the price of oil is high enough they can afford such horrendous costs.

A business plan must call first for the consideration of the question of the market. What will it pay, what does the competition charge? Cost determines the floor on price, while demand and competition determines the more flexible ceiling. In the area of the "flexible ceiling" lies the profit opportunity.

There is seldom sufficient data about the market. The information is hard to extract, published figures are few and unreliable. The prices and discounts offered by competition are sometimes known with precision but are often fudged. Companies keep few records about what happens at different selling prices. Selling prices are changing all the time. It is almost impossible to extract pure "price" from the bundle of services and qualities offered in a competitor's package. Like is seldom compared with like.

Little wonder then that there is virtually no research method that is reliable

---

Figure 3.5
Odd things that happen with pricing

When a U.S. firm charged 37¢ for work gloves, they did not sell. When the price was raised to 39¢, the buyers snapped them up.

Children's shirts were offered for $1.49 each. When the offer was changed to "2 for $3," sales increased 50%.

A British study showed that only 51% of consumers knew the exact price of the seven most frequently bought products.

In the United States 60% of all special offers are bought by only 22% of households.

A sample of consumers had to choose between fictitious, outwardly identical floor polish products, the only difference being the price. 57% of them chose the more expensive product.

According to a reliable sample survey, a consumer's general perception of "a bargain" means that a package of frozen peas must be cheaper by 25%, whereas a "bargain" washing machine needs to be only 15% cheaper than the standard price.

Apparently, people begrudge spending money on some things more than others. High on a "Begrudging Index" were expenditures on electricity, soft drinks and briefcases. Low on the index were bread, margarine and cigarettes.

A Nielsen study of consumer markets showed that price offers of less than 10% had hardly any consumer response, but offers of between 10% and 12% had a correlation between sales in over half the cases recorded. Prices offers above 13% and much higher had distinct relationships with sales effect. But the higher the offer, the less likely it was that the brand would maintain its increased share of the market afterwards.

A Swedish study, repeated in many parts of the world, shows that high price is associated in the consumer's mind with high quality, particularly for product groups involving fashion or taste.

A French study showed that 53% of purchasers would be willing to pay 12,500 francs (old francs) for a radio, whereas only 30% of purchasers would be willing to pay 10,000 francs for the same set.

Another French study showed that price sensitivity to products that are well known is high, whereas the sensitivity to products that are unknown is low.

---

enough, or has applications across most markets sufficiently widespread to tell us with precision "what the market will bear."

Pricing can never be an automatic or impersonal process. It will never be reduced to a mathematical or accounting formula. It is an elusive art. A little theory will help—so will a little courage. Inspiration will help—a creative touch here and there just to give added value that can be presented as an important and unique benefit. That is the means by which prices can be nudged along.

A little luck will help, too. The more you examine the market, the better you will be able to judge the value of what you have to offer against your competition. The more you work out a profit and pricing plan first, and then ensure that costs stay in line, the "luckier" you'll be.

*   *   *

Now go back to the questionnaire at the start of this chapter and complete it again.

Cost-related Pricing Systems | 4

Before reading the chapter, complete the answers to these questions in the spaces on the left-hand side. Then without looking at the answers, read the chapter. Finally, complete the answers again, making any changes you think fit. Score both sets of your answers. This tells you how much the chapter has affected your opinion. Scores are at the end of the book (p. 195).

COSTINGS: QUESTIONS TO TAX STUDENTS OF BUSINESS

Q.1 *Your wife is deeply engrossed in the business of making and selling patchwork quilts in partnership with your neighbor's wife. An argument is raging about how their production should be costed and priced for sale.*

(a) Your wife says, *"We should add up all the hours we spend in making these quilts and things, and cost this on a per hour basis, adding in the costs of the materials we buy for each quilt. Then we should work out how much it costs to run this whole business, including shopping for the material, talking to the customers, as well as advertising, and make an allowance in money terms for all of this, plus the profit we want to make. We can divide this cost by the number of quilts we will sell. This makes sure we will get back all the money and time we have spent in running the business, if we price each quilt accordingly. The price will then cover the money we have spent and the total time we have spent on the business."* *(b)* Your neighbor's wife says, *"No, we should do it another way. I agree that we should put in the price we pay for the materials and the time spent in making the quilts themselves. But it is very difficult to keep a check on the rest of the cost, because both of us fit the time in between doing other jobs. For instance, I bought some material the other day when I was out shopping in the normal way. Now, how can we cost that time in? I say we lump together all the time spent in running the business and divide it up equally among the customers. If we get a big order, we can price it down a lot because it is still only one shopping trip for materials, isn't it?"* *(c)* Your neighbor himself intervenes with another idea. *"Why don't you sell it to the shops on the basis of their giving you back all your basic costs of materials and such like in each of the items they buy, and then get them to add on something extra for all the trouble you've had in getting the work done? The extra can be your profit."* *(d)* It is clear that no one can agree on any one method, so *you* come up with the final idea, which everyone accepts, of course. *"Get the shop to specify exactly what they want by way of materials, colors and such like. Then work out what they themselves would have to pay if they bought the materials and had them made up for themselves by dressmakers at home. See what that cost would be to them; you'll buy the materials cheaper because you can buy in bulk direct from the wholesaler, and your workers are very efficient, so it*

won't cost you as much. Then work out what you think the shop will be prepared to pay you for the quilts. That's your price. It is up to you whether you make money or not. And if you don't make money, have you thought about breeding hamsters instead? Now, there's a good sideline."

Four techniques of pricing have been described here. Who was using

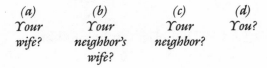

(a)	*(b)*	*(c)*	*(d)*
Your wife?	*Your neighbor's wife?*	*Your neighbor?*	*You?*

Q.2

    Marginal pricing

    Standard cost pricing

    Product analysis pricing

    Cost-plus-profit pricing

    Check correct answer.

Score   **Score**

____   ____

       Before reading chapter.   *After reading chapter.*

____   ____

Q.2   *Marginal pricing can be used to explain away any deal which gives us a positive contribution to overhead and profit, even though the deal may be agreed at just above variable costs of production.*

    When would you use a marginal pricing deal of this nature?

                                                      Yes   No

    (a) *When you want to clear excess stocks?*

    (b) *When you want to impress a favorite long-standing customer?*

    (c) *When you can dump the product overseas?*

    (d) *When you are at full pcoduction capacity?*

    (e) *When you can get cash in exchange?*

Score   **Score**

____   ____

       Before reading chapter.   *After reading chapter.*

____   ____

Q.3 *How far do you agree with the following statements?*

Yes   No   Sometimes

(a) *You can use the cost data in your bud-
getary control system and in your tax
returns for your basic costing data for the
purpose of pricing.*

(b) *Every product should yield a predeter-
mined satisfactory profit in the short run.*

(c) *Would you charge different prices to customers who cost about the same to serve?*

(d) *A standard mechanical formula that
everyone understands is best for pricing
purposes.*

(e) *An accountant deals only with things that
can be measured accurately. That's why
he should not be asked to produce net
profit estimates for individual products.*

(f) *If companies paid more attention to what
the accountants say and gave them better
data they would get a better result.*

(g) *If you lower the price you'll sell more.*

Score   **Score**

_____   _____

Before reading chapter.   After reading chapter.

_____   _____

Scores
Some of these are difficult.

Above 18	Very good.
12–17	In the majority.
Below 12	No disgrace. The questions are quite com-plicated.

Cost-related Pricing Systems | 4

Perhaps your ears really *are* different. You may be one of the very small minority of people who have perfect pitch. That could cause you to enter the market for hi-fi equipment.

In most markets there is a reverse demand curve towards the floor price. The lowest priced products seldom outsell the others. If the lowest priced suppliers could find a way to improve their price and quality (and usually their distribution system as well) they would sell more. That is particularly true of markets involving fashion or taste.

Most people believe that they can distinguish minute differences in sound quality, but it is very difficult to demonstrate. Within different segments of the hi-fi market, manufacturers compete fiercely with technological differences that are very difficult, sometimes almost impossible for the average human ear to measure.

To improve the sound quality of hi-fi equipment you must have a good match between the amplifier (the interesting area for advanced electronics) and the speakers (the dull area for the electronics engineer). For most people to improve the sound of their hi-fi unit they should upgrade their speakers, to match the amplifier. But the electronics engineers enjoy working on amplifiers and tuners.

If the man in the street were asked to distinguish the sound quality between two different hi-fi units in the same market segment he would find great difficulty in picking out the better one. But if he were told the price of the two units before coming to his decision he would pick the higher priced unit as providing him with the better sound.

Expectation plays a large part in perception, and a unit which is known to be expensive will invariably "sound better."

Whiskey drinkers, cigarette smokers, butter eaters—all of them find it practically impossible to tell their own regular brand apart from the rest if you subject them to a blind test. There are hundreds of product fields where that is true. But if you show them different prices during the blind test then their "senses" will detect differences in quality.

Often when looking at cost-related systems of pricing, the idea of what is "morally" right enters the mind. People do have different limits on this issue. When people feel their profits are too high, then they either give extra away for nothing, or they deliberately incur greater cost than is strictly necessary. The former phenomenon is known to sales managers as "buying back the business." Salesmen often add in extras for nothing, after the deal has been done, and it

40

has nothing to do with establishing goodwill. The salesman feels guilty about the size of the order or the profit he has made. The latter phenomenon is known to production managers as "over engineering." A master baker in a pie factory always used 10% more fat than was used in other factories. "We make a lot of profit here with these new machines," he said. "And the fat adds to the quality of the pastry." It did not matter that blind product tests by the market research manager could prove beyond the shadow of a doubt that no one in the market could discern the difference in pastry quality. The master baker was wasting $25,000 a year in extra costs, just because he felt guilty about making money from his new machines.

> Advice: *If your costomers are happy and you are keeping people employed and telling the truth, then don't ever feel guilty about how much money you are making. This is called capitalism.*

STANDARD COST PRICING

This is a lovely, logical system, which most companies use and which does not work at all well, but they seldom find that out. There is something to be said for it but not a lot. The company uses cost "standards" based upon management accounting systems. The variable costs of production are added up, principally costs of materials and direct labor, or bought-in components. Total costs are divided by the number of units to be produced, thus providing a variable cost per unit.

The total costs of running the organization are added up—the factory building, the management and administrative staff, the running expenses of the business over a given time period. Those costs are divided by the number of units to be sold in that period. That becomes the fixed cost per unit. The profit required over the same time is added in to the calculation on a per unit basis.

Adding together the variable cost, the fixed cost and the profit per unit provides a selling price. Nothing could be simpler, except that it is an inferior method of setting prices.

The first problem is that it assumes that costs are the thing which cause people to buy. But the market is not the least bit interested in cost. It is interested in getting what it wants at a competitive price.

The next question is, who should benefit from your efficiency? You should. Using the standard cost system, full cost accounting, full cost pricing, call it what you will, if your fixed costs are treated on a percentage basis, then if you manage to get your fixed costs down your selling prices go down. You reap no advantage. Actually, you will lose by it, because the profit is usually calculated on a percentage basis also.

> Proverb for cost accountants: *Profits are made out of total cash in, minus total cash out. No one ever found a dollar bill in a percentage.*

As your selling price goes down, so will your actual profit per unit (but not your magic percentage).

Figure 4.1
A three-step guide to standard costing

STEP 1.   Set up a system of "standard" costs based on an assumed "normal" rate of output over a number of years. All fixed and variable costs should be added, and the total divided by the number of units to be produced. That gives you the average cost per unit. The following costs should be included.

(a) Cost to design (include building and testing preproduct prototype, if appropriate)
(b) Production (labor and materials)
(c) Depreciation on research and development and plant investments
(d) Overhead
(e) Rent
(f) Insurance
(g) Handling and packaging
(h) Storage
(i) Cost of building and carrying inventory
(j) Advertising expenses (assuming you use a percentage of sales for determining advertising budget)
(k) Delivery
(l) Installation, services
(m) Warranty-service costs
(n) Patent royalty

STEP 2.   To total cost add a set percentage of cost (based on experience) to cover selling, merchandising and administration costs, plus a "normal" profit, to arrive at a preliminary price.

STEP 3.   Compare preliminary price with the going market price for a similar product, and adjust slightly if needed.

A further problem is that using the standard cost system, if you produce products at too high a cost, compared to competition, then you will have to reduce your price anyway—because your product will not sell. But if you produce products below the cost of your competition, then the market will not tell you that you are too cheap. Have you ever heard a buyer tell you that he will voluntarily give you more money on account of your efficiency? And you will not *necessarily* sell more, just because you are cheaper.

Another problem is, if you call your factory labor a "variable" cost, that assumes that if you sell 10% more than planned, then you will employ 10% more labor. But you won't. You'll keep your existing labor and give them overtime rates. If your sales go down by 10% less than forecast, then the assumption is that your labor bill will go down by 10%. But it won't. Try firing 10% of your staff one week, and putting them back the next.

But there are more problems. The entire system is based upon forecast sales. But how do you know how many sales you are going to get? And will your sales be affected by your price? Yes, they will.

As living proof of the fact that standard costing systems are weak for pricing purposes, just have a look at any multiproduct company using the system. Once the products are launched and on the market, the market and the competition take over. Are products taken off the market when their magical "gross profit" margin is seen to be eroded? No, they are not. Are radical new products given the same costing treatment as well-established products in the same range, with all the overhead of research and development charged to the new products? No, they are not.

If multiproduct companies priced in that way, they would soon build up prices to enormous levels. So they fudge their own figures. They give new products a free ride on the distribution system for one year. ("Our trucks are calling there anyway.") They write off their research and development charges. ("The costs are all sunk now anyway.") They write off the general management contribution. ("It's the established products that keep the business going. These new ones are for the future.") This, despite the fact that general management has spent a horrendous proportion of its time and cost on the new product.

And notice that in giving the new products an easy ride on the costs, they are creating even heavier burdens for the existing procucts to bear. The big-selling existing lines are nearly always more profitable than they appear to be from the costings.

Standard cost pricing is inflexible. It is anachronistic. It is based upon a historical view of past costs leading to tomorrow's prices. It is altogether a weak system to use, but on the other hand, it may be a less weak costing system than any of the others that follow. To provide a base-line figure, standard costing may be acceptable. To measure profitability, standard costing may be acceptable. But to rely on it, *and on nothing else*, to set selling prices is completely unacceptable. Yet many companies do just that.

COST-PLUS-PROFIT SYSTEMS OF PRICING

Now, this is a much healthier system, because at least you may be guaranteed to stay in business. (If you can get your customers to sign a blank check for you, then please send me your name and address so that I can buy shares in your company.) The system has the great virtue of flexibility.

As a management consultant you are facing your client. "How much will it cost?" he asks you. "$75 an hour plus out-of-pocket expenses at cost," you reply, "How many hours?" he wants to know. "How do I know that until I've done the work?" you say. "Ah," he muses—and loses.

"What's this mileage charge you've given me—$225 for a journey from New

Figure 4.2
Drawbacks of cost-plus pricing

→ Difficult, in advance, to determine such costs as construction, material price changes, and similar costs.

→ Difficult to allocate joint costs to specific products

→ Not based on realistic profit goal or market share objective

→ Ignores elasticity of demand

→ Generally disregards competition

→ Buyer is more concerned about the cost and value of product to him than about production and selling costs to supplier

→ Doesn't distinguish between out-of-pocket and "sunk" costs*

→ Difficult to determine "fair return"

→ Ignores capital requirements and return on investment

→ Many costs vary with volume, and volume depends on price charged

*Those that are spent, regardless of production level.

York to Washington in your car?" he demands. "Well, I've got this Porsche and the depreciation, plus tax, plus interest payments, plus insurance, plus gas, oil and repairs, works out to $1.00 a mile. You see, I don't drive many miles in it. And you agreed to repay my expenses, didn't you?" you reply. "Ah," he muses — and loses.

Cost-plus-profit formulas disguise many inefficiencies in costs. They also leave too many gaps in the measurement of costs. How do you cost out delivery? Just cost the journey there? Or do you include the empty journey back as well? Do you add the selling cost to the calculation — or is it included in the profit?

In many types of business, cost-plus-profit formulas are the only sensible way to contract for business. Big deals can often be handled that way. IBM in London has a deal with a major hotel chain. Its visiting executives stay in a certain hotel at special "cost-plus" rates. The contract is valuable to the hotel group, but IBM insists on examining the quarterly profit and loss accounts from the hotel. That makes it very difficult to manipulate invoices. When selling, then, companies using cost-plus-profit formulas like to identify every possible item of cost, and that leads to tortuous accounting and calculation, particularly with semivariable costs such as repairs and renewals or delivery costs, which rise and fall with significant changes in the level of production but are not directly associated with every small change in the level. When buying under this system, companies like to be able to identify and verify costs for themselves. But they must take care that they are not being charged with someone else's costs, and that they are not subsidizing a wasteful production system.

MARGINAL PRICING

If cost-plus-profit will generally keep you in business, then this can easily put you out of it. Marginal pricing provides the intellectual rationale for accepting

---

Figure 4.3
Marginal pricing

The basic theory of marginal pricing is that price is set at a point where marginal costs equals marginal revenue.

Marginal cost is the increase in total cost as a result of producing and selling one more unit of product. Below, you can see that from zero production up to a volume of X, marginal cost decreases; then begins to increase. X represents the point where economies of scale have been exceeded. After that point, marginal costs tend to increase.

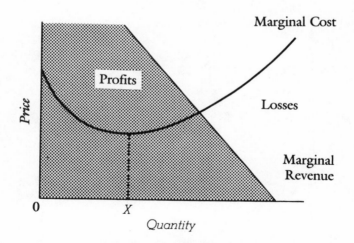

Marginal *revenue* is the additional amount received as a result of selling one more unit of a product. Note that marginal revenue decreases as quantity increases. That is because of the supply and demand theory that people will buy greater quantities of a product at lower prices.

Figure 4.4
Marginal Cost example

1 *Production level*	2 *Total fixed cost*	3 *Total variable cost*	4 *Total cost* *(column 2 + column 3)*	5 *Marginal cost* (The amount by which each successive cost exceeds the previous cost)
0	40	0	40	—
1	40	60	100	60
2	40	112	152	52
3	40	155	195	43
4	40	189	229	34
5	40	205	245	25

the lowest possible price, and is exceptionally dangerous when uncontrolled. Every weak salesman, when faced by a big buyer who is squeezing him hard on the price, will come back to his management with something like the following argument:

"This buyer is not going to pay our full price for this big order because he can get it cheaper elsewhere. Do we want to do the business or not? If we give him a price reduction, then we are making some money on the deal, over and above our variable costs. Would you rather have this money, or would you rather not have it?"

Faced with such logic, a manager under pressure will usually agree that it is better to do the low price deal than none at all.

> *Salesmen will give you a million reasons for a marginal price deal. There is only one defense. "If we did all our deals like that, we'd be out of business." And that is true.*

The problem concerns a misconception about costs. The costs of making the product include the materials and other variable costs, but they also include the costs of running the business as a whole, salaries, rents, administration and the like. All of those costs must be recovered in the long run by all the deals that are done.

Marginal pricing throws all of those fixed costs into a pot called "Contribution to overhead and profit."

THE COST ARGUMENTS COMPARED

Suppose you are a mountain guide in the Alps. A client asks you to take a party of two of them to Mont Blanc, and you give him your price per head. When they turn up, there are three of them, not two. They argue that the price should be no more than for two because it is not costing you any more to take the third member of the party. They are using the marginal cost argument. If you argue that taking three adds to the total time for the journey, they might then agree to give you a little more money to compensate for that. They, and you, are still using the marginal cost argument. You can see how dangerous the marginal cost argument can be. If you did all your deals like this, then on every party you guide, you will be charging fully for only one person—the first. All the others are getting a nearly free ride.

No, as a mountain guide you explain that the cost to you is your total income for a season, divided by the number of people you expect to guide during the season. Everyone must pay the same rate. On some trips you make money (the large parties) but those compensate for the trips where you lose money (single people). The full costs are not the cost of a particular journey, but the entire cost of all the journeys. That's the full cost or standard cost argument.

You could, of course, solve the problem by changing your pricing base so as to avoid such arguments about numbers. You could charge on a per journey basis regardless of the number of people you take. But that would make you very expensive for a single client, and would inundate you with large parties who are getting you cheaply.

So the actual costing system you use does matter a great deal in practice. Mountain guides don't work it out like that, of course. They set standard charges for particular routes and for the numbers in the party depending upon the popularity of the route, combined with their own desire to do it. On very difficult routes, some guides refuse to go. But other guides, including a few of the world's top climbers, have been known to do such routes for nothing, because they want to do them. That is the ultimate in marginal cost—doing it for nothing.

When the Alpine guide also owns a farm in Chamonix, and his wife runs a guest house, how is he to allocate his costs between his different sources of income? He cannot sensibly do it. And if he tries to allocate his fixed costs between different sources of income, when he compares the results to another guide's costing, they will be found to be totally different in their allocations. If both parties now proceed to price their services according to their costs, they will get different results. And which of their clients will care that the charge for a route has been influenced by the fact that one guide spends 30% of his time on his vegetable garden, while another spends 20% of his time on his chickens? The clients don't care at all. And if the guide happens to get the price of his guided climbs right for the market, then his price for eggs will be wrong.

Strangely enough, it is this very confusion that causes the marginal costing system to be used. Because of the difficulty in identifying and allocating fixed costs across a very wide range of different income sources (to which of your own products and services would you charge the time of your secretary?), companies add up the total of the variable costs they can identify, add in any other semidirect costs they can trace to the particular activity, and then bundle the rest into a general contribution figure toward overhead and net profit. How do they do this? By sheer guesswork, based upon a view of what the market will bear, what the competition is charging and how much they want the work.

WHEN YOU SHOULD NEVER USE MARGINAL PRICING

If you are going to consider a marginal price, well below your full costs, then these are the principal factors to take into account. *Never* do it if it will set a precedent for the long run with your big customers. *Never* do it if the news of the low price deal will spread in the market and other customers will want the same. *Never* do it if it commits you to extra capital cost in the short run, or in the long run. *Never* do it if it uses up scarce resources you need elsewhere. *Never* do it if you have to sacrifice some full profit business to fit it in. *Never* do it if it costs you cash flow as well, by giving credit. *Never* do it if it will undermine the position of you or your salesmen in the market. *Never* delegate discretion on marginal prices down the line.

IF YOU MUST DO A MARGINAL COST DEAL

Dump the product or service well away from your usual market, and away from your usual customers. Clear your excess inventory. Turn it into a cash-up-front deal. Keep a particular competitor under pressure in his own backyard—but be careful because he might do the same to you. Do it on a once-only basis; repeat business should be done at normal prices. Make sure that one person controls all the marginal price decisions.

Here is an example of a sensible way to operate marginal pricing in a business. A packaging company hired a new chief operating officer. He found chaos in the pricing and costing department. Everyone seemed to be pleading special reasons for every major contract. The standard cost schedules were seldom maintained, the adverse revenue variances were very high, and the company was losing money.

It took him three years to become fully effective, but by the end of that time he had the company changed around. He made everyone produce budgets for their expenditures against a forecast of sales—normal procedure in all companies. The forecast of sales was broken down by product type into units of sale at standard price. Discount schedules were set up for special categories of customer and for large volume orders. They reflected the realities of the market place. The entire company budget was drawn up and agreed to against a profit

---

Figure 4.5
How to make losses easily

This example shows a company with an ordinary cost structure which first of all loses only 5% of its sales volume, and then finds that it has underestimated inflation by 5%. At this point the management agrees to drop its price by 5% in order to win back sales volume, but unbeknownst to them, so do all the competitors at the same time. Market shares, therefore, hold level and the following is the result:

	Original cost structure	Losing 5% sales volume	Costs up by 5%	Extra 5% discount
Sales	100	95	95	90.25
Direct costs	50	47.5	} 91.875	91.875
Indirect costs	40	40		91.875
Net profit	10	7.5	3.125	(1.625 loss)
% change in net profit		−25%	−67%	−116%

objective for the business as a whole. The company was organized to produce a result against the budget. So far, the managing director had done nothing unusual for a normal company.

But once he had the company running profitably against the budget, he made the production and engineering personnel identify where spare capacity lay and at what times of the year. Having identified the idle assets in the business, he put an accountant together with a senior marketing executive and a technical executive. Those three were charged with the task of selling off the idle capacity on a marginal price basis. But they had to work within severe constraints of policy.

First of all, they were not allowed to produce and sell any product if it would compete with their normal products in the normal market. Next, they were not allowed to sell spare capacity to their existing customers, so that normal relationships would not be damaged. Third, the company was not prepared to commit any capital expenditure to selling the spare capacity unless it was entirely recovered out of the price. The company was not prepared to sell spare capacity if it tied up their funds. Generally, such special deals had to be on a one-only basis, with cash up front. You may argue that their hands were tied so tight that it was impossible for the three people to move the spare capacity. Yet it was done, and done very effectively. The company never forgot that, basically, it earned its money on the normal business to which everyone was committed. This marginal business was for convenience only. It could be chopped off in a moment. It was treated just as a little extra on to the profit. Actually, it made quite a lot of extra money for the company—doubled their net profit in fact (but that, of course, depends upon how you treat it in the costings). If marginal pricing is treated as a small part of the overall business and is kept strapped down so that it does not contaminate normal business done at normal prices, then marginal pricing has a role to play.

THE PROPER ROLE OF COSTS IN PRICING

No one is suggesting that we abandon costing procedures in a business—that would be a ludicrous proposition. What is being promoted hard is the idea that costs alone should not determine selling prices.

In practice you can drive a huge wedge in practically every system of cost pricing. One practical example will suffice. The Swedish giant SKF makes the finest antifriction bearings in the world. It competes with FAG from Germany, Ina from Italy, and the Japanese for markets all over the world. Its production of bearings is specialized in different factories. No two factories make the same bearings. So the customers for each factory's output are the company's own sales offices around the world. Facing the customers, SKF sales engineers must produce a logically consistent price list. Bearings of similar size and quality must show similar prices, even though they may be produced in different factories. Two similar bearings will have different labor costs, markedly different overhead costs, and massively different transport costs. Not only that, but the factories receive their revenue in their local currency so that the transfer pricing system between different divisions must allow for currency equalization. There is no way in which a true cost-plus standard profit pricing system can be applied to every bearing. It would produce a ludicrous price list. What happens in practice? The market takes over and becomes the determining factor for the selling price.

But the company still needs its costing system to show which products make money and which do not make money. Costs are needed to evaluate the profitability of the assortment. The sales offices must be encouraged to push the products that show high profits or that the factories need to fill up their production lines. The sales offices must know which are the least profitable products for the company, so that they can be held back. That is the proper role of costs in the pricing mechanism: to show how much money is being made, what is profitable and what is not profitable.

The danger in costing systems is the use of percentages to indicate "profitability." Just because one product produces a "profit" of 45% does not mean that it is more profitable than another which produces 35%. This is a very difficult idea for some people to understand, particularly if they have been working under that assumption all their lives. Costs will show you the total amount of money earned by the company in each sector of the business, after deducting from the income. That is the profit, the total amount of money (*not* the percentage).

PRODUCT ANALYSIS PRICING: A TECHNIQUE FOR BIDDING[8]

Many companies produce nonstandard products that are custom-built or suited to a particular local market. Local market conditions might be changeable, and competition erratic. So the company's pricing decision will have to be taken down the line at the local level.

The decision is always difficult because the buyer is usually expert. He specifies clearly his requirements and submits them to companies for tender.

He will select the quotation which is around the lowest, from among those companies meeting the specifications. So the buyer's position is very powerful.

In this case, your pricing decision must be market-oriented. This requires a target price to be set initially, based upon your need for the work, the volume of the order, and the likely level of competitive bids. The actual price to be quoted should be a little higher than this, to allow for maneuver.

A pricing data sheet is prepared showing the allowance for materials, for bought-in components, and for any special features required. These are all costed at the market value, i.e., the sum which the customer would pay for these things if buying himself.

This sum is compared with the deals which have been done by your company in the recent past over similar product groups. The figures are compared and discussed with sales, and the target price is selected.

Finally, the decision to bid. At the selected target price, are you better off taking the job or refusing it? To answer that you must consider the alternatives.

Do you have an alternative use for the production capacity; or will it lie idle? Will taking the job tie you up in some way so that you will be unable to take on other more profitable work?

How much will this contract provide for future business with this customer, what prestige will the contract bring, and so on? The system has the advantage of flexibility. It handles nonstandard production well. It looks principally at the market, particularly in the form of past evidence of similar work, to see what jobs have been won or lost at what prices. It takes account of how much you need the work, and how much volume is involved in the deal. It sets limits for costs. It is quick and it avoids the abominations of percentages.

What happens in practice is that the sales people work to their target price. Their target line would be 100. They have personal discretion to go down as low as 95 on a particular deal. Their sales manager can go lower, to 90. On a big deal, the VP of sales has discretion down to, say, 65 of the target price.

But the sales people must balance their low price deals with high price deals. They are expected and encouraged to go to 125 of their target price, if the customer can stand it, if the order is not price-sensitive. Refurbishment work, for example, will generally stand a much higher price than target, and it helps to balance the very low prices which might be obtained from original equipment manufacturers for the supply of component parts in bulk. (See W. Brown and E. Jacques, Product Analysis Pricing, Heinemann, 1965.)

SUMMARY

Costs are never what they seem to be. Put two different management accountants on to the same costing problem without any preconceptions or agreed-upon rules, and they will come up with different answers—unless you let them talk to each other first, in which case their answers will agree to the third decimal place.

Standard costing is the usual system upon which prices are based in most companies. No one is against companies preparing their costs. Business cannot be run properly without such systems. But as a sole means of settling prices, the system is full of flaws. Let the standard cost price be the *lowest* unit price you are willing to accept. That is a good starting point; but then add margins to it. If the standard cost throws out prices which are too high, then the market will find you out, and you will have to reduce them or pull out of the market. So it will seldom price things too high for the long run. But it often does price things too low—and the market never tells you that. Even strong sales figures will not reveal that the price is too low—they could be strong for a host of reasons, and low price does not necessarily mean big volume orders—unless the price is very much lower than the average.

Marginal pricing works only if you can guarantee that the whole costs of your entire business can be covered by your normal sales at full selling prices. Then you can use a marginal price if you want. The problem occurs when it is very difficult to establish a stnadard cost system, because the fixed costs in the

Figure 4.6
How prices can collapse quickly in capital-intensive industries

In the cement industry in Westphalia, new manufacturing processes resulted in much lower costs, but created larger manufacturing capacity and very high fixed costs. In the early sixties a kiln had a capacity of 200 tons output per day, and ten years later 2,000-ton kilns were built. A government ban on the price cartel between the main producers, combined with the need to fill the spare capacity, caused the companies to drop the price of cement from $15.00. Ultimately it fell to less than $7.00 per ton, which was well below the cost of production. Small and medium-sized firms went out of business.

In Europe the market for integrated circuits (semi-conductors) was dominated by companies such as Motorola, Philips, and Siemens. In 1963 the prices were $25.00 per unit, in 1965 they were down to $12.50 per unit, and in 1967 they were $2.50 per unit. Over capacity in the market caused prices to collapse again in 1970, when the prices came down to $0.65 each (B. Hake, *Hazards of Growth*, 1974).

business are a very high proportion of the total costs and they are very difficult to allocate between different products or services. Then you may have to cost out variables, add on a margin for luck to cover your overhead, and that's your selling price. Dangerous, as you can see, but sometimes unavoidable, particularly when accountants are employed under a strict department head who will not allow them to make sensible guesses about overhead allocations. "That's for the crystal-ball merchants in the marketing department," says the chief management accountant. "Only record what you can measure exactly." It's a bit Jesuitical, and not very helpful.

Paying for the actual costs of production plus an agreed allowance for profit, on very large orders—defense contracts for example, or local government work—may be one way to cover the costs and stay in business. It appeals to the customer's sense of morality, but he will want to see the justification for the figures just the same. The system can disguise a great deal of skulduggery in the presentation of the data, and can hide a lot of waste.

Product analysis pricing shows what the customer would have to pay if he arranged to have the product made for himself. It sets a target for costs and a target for price. It uses past pricing and bidding data, and is an excellent system for a jobbing business such as a printer to use. Most companies have an element of jobbing work somewhere in their production process, and there the analysis system can be very useful.

*   *   *

Now go back to the questionnaire at the start of this chapter and complete it again.

Market-related Pricing Systems | 5

Before reading the chapter, complete the answers to these questions in the spaces on the left-hand side. Then without looking at the answers, read the chapter. Finally, complete the answers again, making any changes you think fit. Score both sets of your answers. This tells you how much the chapter has affected your opinion. Scores are at the end of the book (p.196).

AWKWARD QUESTIONS FOR MARKETING MANAGERS

Q.1 *You are a marketing manager in a pharmaceutical company. You make a life-support drug. Once people are treated with it, they must stay on it continuously to survive. It has been outdated by a machine which now treats new patients. So gradually your market is eroding. You sell very little of the drug, which is costly to produce.*
 Which pricing technique would you use?

(a) A pricing system based upon cost-plus; (b) a pricing system based upon what the market will bear; (c) a pricing system based upon a notion of "morality"; (d) a pricing system based upon what competition charges.

Score   **Score**
_____   _____

    Before reading chapter.   *After reading chapter.*

_____   _____

Q.2 *You have just bought some fashionable sandals from an Italian importer. They are the latest thing in chic fashion. If you take your normal shop margins you would sell them at $50.*
 How would you price them (they are unique in style for your market)?
(a) $50; (b) $48; (c) $59.95; (d) $47.95 plus heavy price promotion; (e) $64.95.

Score   **Score**
_____   _____

    Before reading chapter.   *After reading chapter.*

_____   _____

Q.3 *You like making money. You buy well and sell at good prices. But everyone makes a mistake sometimes. You have excess inventory of a poor line to clear. You must move it out to create cash to allow you to buy a better line. What's your view of promotional pricing?*

(a) Actively encourage it all the time; (b) offer it only to your best customers; (c) refuse to use it at all; (d) use it sparingly, outside your normal markets; (e) use it a little, but make it look as if you use it a lot with advertising, etc.

Score   **Score**

_____   _____

Before reading chapter.   *After reading chapter.*

_____   _____

Q.4   *If you want to price aggressively in order to take over the major part of the whole market, what level of price discount should you be thinking of offering in a normal consumer product market, as a minimum discount to make the market turn over to you in a serious way?*

(a) 10% off competitors' prices; (b) 15% off competitors' prices; (c) 20% off competitors' prices; (d) 30% off competitors' prices; (e) between 40% and 50% off competitors' prices.

Score   **Score**

_____   _____

Before reading chapter.   *After reading chapter.*

_____   _____

Q.5   *If you average out all the sales of the products in a consumer market at different prices, then you can arrive at an "average" price for all the products in the market. Yours is the biggest selling brand in the market; you and your nearest two competitors share about 60% of the whole market between you. When measured against the "average" market price, where would you expect your brand leader product to be positioned?*

(a) 10% under the average price; (b) on or closely around the average price; (c) 20% under the average price; (d) 7% above the average price.

Score   **Score**

_____   _____

Before reading chapter.   *After reading chapter.*

_____   _____

Scores

Above 20	Very good.
14–19	In with the crowd.
8–13	Go on, try.
7 or less	Are we talking about the same subject?

For 45 years one company alone has held the printing contract for the 3.3 million copies which are sold each week of a national magazine. The order is huge, absolutely enormous. Most major printers in the world would love to get it. For many years it was impossible for a competitor to steal the contract away because of the pricing system used.

Throughout that time, the printers sold their work on a straight cost-plus basis. The customer agreed to a notional level of "profit" which he would judge to be ethical, and beyond that he would agree to pay the printers their costs of production. The customer thought he was getting a good deal for his corporation. The printer knew he was getting a good deal for his own company, because the nature of the agreement guaranteed that the printer would make a profit—whatever inefficiencies he might have.

But things changed. A seven-year contract was agreed upon on a normal basis in competition with other bids, with the supplier looking after his own costs. Within weeks, the supplier found that, in order to make a profit, he would have to lay off nearly one-fifth of his staff. He also found that he could do so and still produce the work at the same standard of quality as before with some new investment in equipment. Imagine the unseen waste in the previous deal when spread over 45 years!

There was a major strike, of course, over the layoffs, but that is another story.

Morality is an idea that often enters people's minds when prices are discussed—it is one of a series of market-related pricing systems which are sometimes used. When an organization favors a particular pricing system, it seldom does so to the exclusion of all other systems. With market-related systems, the costs are calculated also and usually form the company's floor price.

MORAL PRICING

"Fishermen don't have a lot of money to spend so I try to give them a fair deal. We give them really good value. That's the way things should be." This is a cafe proprietor at a marina speaking. He sells at low prices because of his notion of what is "right" for his customers. That differs from penetration pricing, where prices are deliberately low in order to capture the major share of the market.

Figure 5.1
Market-related pricing systems

Pricing system	*Purpose*
"Moral" pricing	Based upon a notion of justice and fairness
Pricing points	Easing through psychological price barriers
Promotional pricing	Used as the basis for forcing the sales of the product
Skimming the market	Slicing off the top segment of demand with high prices
Prestige pricing	The psychology of using extremely high price to add a special appeal
Penetration pricing	To force high market share through low prices

"Moral" pricing is used principally by monopolist organizations such as local and national government, and institutions, where costs are particularly difficult to identify, and where the subject may be socially or politically sensitive.

For example, the faculty of a certain university met with the representatives of labor unions in order to discuss how a proposed child care facility was to be priced. Five different price levels were agreed upon—one level for single parent families (the lowest), one level for married students, another level for members of the faculty, and so on. The prices were all based upon an idea of affordability and justice. They had hardly anything to do with cost.

Suppose a municipal transit authority suffers a loss. A new mayor is elected and announces that the transit fares are to be reduced by 25%. It is "right" to do this, he says, because the ordinary person without a car cannot afford high fares. To pay for this fare reduction, the taxpayers of this city face higher taxes. Why them? Because, the argument runs, they can afford it and it is "right" that they should subsidize public transportation.

Question: *How high does profit have to be before it is immoral?*

There is no judgment intended as to good or bad, right or wrong on these issues; in many cases the pricing problem is so complex that a notion of what is just and fair is the only way to do it. This idea is particularly prevalent in socialist countries and systems.

Question: *If the price is so low that we suffer losses and have to fire staff, is that more moral?*

Around the world there are many organizations that cannot price up to what the market will bear because of their philosophy. Charity organizations will often price their everyday functions and products low. But when they run a special event to attract the wealthy, then they price the tickets to their "all-star" functions very high indeed, because they are appealing to rich people "who can afford it."

For example, there are youth hostels to be found in most countries of the world. They provide simple forms of accommodation for those who want to enjoy the countryside, and their aim is to price low in order to offer facilities for people with little money, such as students. With the growth of backpacking and other forms of travel, youth hostels in the most popular areas are packed— reserved for months ahead, sometimes up to a year for a holiday period. A normal commercial organization would reduce some of the demand by pushing up their prices and improving their facilities. But this would undermine the very basis upon which the youth hostels organizations were set up in the first place. They are limited in their ability to push their prices to the limit by their value judgment of "the right price."

The problems associated with a "moral price" system are caused by the fact that many such prices are so low as to make an organization unprofitable, so it pushes other prices up higher to compensate. Or the services and facilities may suffer because there are insufficient funds to pay for their maintenance and renewal. The decisions are based upon individual judgment, notoriously suspect when committees are involved. It also involves the exercise of power or pa- tronage by a monopolist supplier—always an unhealthy basis for morality.

PRICING POINTS

Many industries use pricing points, particularly in distribution trades. If you want to sell a nine-ounce bottle of quality shampoo to a chain drug store, then you will price it to allow the buyer a percentage margin if he sells it in his shops at 98¢ per bottle. If you want to get extra displays and more sales effort from his managers, then you will have to offer the buyer a promotional discount whereby he can sell it at 78¢. He will not sell it at 90¢ nor at 80¢. He wants to get below the next pricing point.

It happens with contracts at large prices also. A contract which should be costed at just over $10 million for a short section of new road, may be submitted at $9.95 million just to get it under the psychological price barrier. And it works; it works really well. Look out for pricing points in your own price lists. If you are in the habit of rounding off your quotations to even sums, then stop it. Shave the price to just below the round figure so that the first digit they read is lower than the one you were planning.

Pricing points are often difficult to handle. Notice that if you want to promote your shampoo down to a selling price of 78¢ in the shop, you may have to cut your selling price to the buyer by 20%—that's a big, big price cut. So what you might do is to introduce a different bottle size of perhaps six ounces in order that the shopkeeper can sell at his 78¢ pricing point and you still make your money. Then, of course, you will get fragmentation of the market by size, and the retailers will complain. You then have to force them to take your full size range. Life can be difficult with this system, particularly in small unit sizes and prices. Your only consolation is that life can be difficult with any other pricing system also.

PROMOTIONAL PRICING

Promotional pricing systems can be used by companies to fill up slack demand. For example, it is much cheaper to use the telephone for making calls on weekends, or during the evening, than it is to use the telephone at the peak hours of weekday mornings. You can get cheaper vacations in major hotels outside of the main summer season. You can fly cheaper if you fly standby. You can get an excursion fare on most airlines which is very cheap, but the terms of which are so constructed that the ticket is almost impossible to use by a businessman making a journey. This kind of demand from businessmen is inelastic—they must travel anyway, whatever the price (almost). But the discretionary demand can be teased out by the use of discount price advantages.

Promotional pricing can be used by retailers and manufacturers to force the market either to sell more, to hold their market position or to make more profit for someone. In Britain the Monopolies Commission, after four years of investigation in the early 1980s, cleared a number of supermarket chains of the charge of abusing their power to force extra discounts from manufacturers. But they acknowledged that giving heavy discounts could be anticompetitive in some cases, and could reduce competition in the long term. That may be true, when promotional competitive pricing is taken to extreme, as evidenced by the fact that one baking company had to pull out of bread production when they were faced with demands for extra discounts of up to 30%. In a low margin item such as bread, the profit margins were too thin to stand this discounting level.

Promotional pricing techniques are also used to clear special problems of excess inventories and low selling lines. Each year, winter and summer, the clothing trade and the department stores hold their sales. The sales started originally as a means whereby retailers sold their out-of-season lines, their ends of style ranges, their awkward sizes. But the whole system became so profitable that nowadays the shops and stores negotiate to buy in "specials" and actively buy for their sales twice a year from suppliers who often make special sale lines as well as clearing their own inventories. The discounts offered in the sale are often 30% or more on the usual prices, but large sales volume is moved in a short period of time. For many groups of shops, if it snows in January, and rains in July, they lose money on the whole year's trading. They've lost the sales that they depend upon for their profit.

The advice on using promotional pricing is, in general: Don't use it unless you are forced to use it. Find some other way to clear your problem. Dump

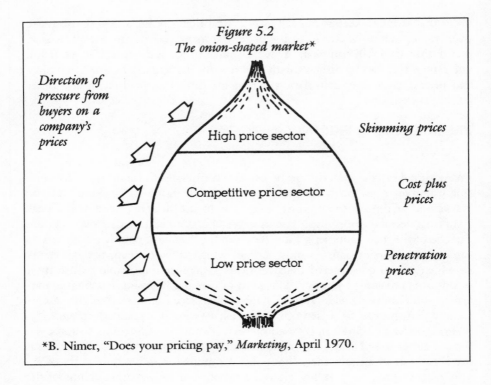

Figure 5.2
*The onion-shaped market**

Direction of
pressure from
buyers on a
company's
prices

High price sector

Skimming prices

Competitive price sector

Cost plus prices

Low price sector

Penetration prices

*B. Nimer, "Does your pricing pay," *Marketing*, April 1970.

the excess inventory in markets outside your mainstream markets if you can. If you succeed with your discount pricing, you will encourage your competitors to follow suit, so in the end everyone sells the same as before but at lower profit. And you will encourage buyers to shop around for better "deals"; you will make your salesmen's job more difficult because they will find themselves unable to sell unless they can offer a special price. You will encourage your customers to switch from paying the full price to paying the discount price.

If you want to get a plane ticket to New York guaranteed for a particular day, reserve an ordinary ticket. Then, on the day of the flight, try to get a standby ticket. If you fail because the flight is sold out, you use your ordinary ticket. If you succeed, you can cancel your ordinary ticket and save the money. The airlines have a way of dealing with this by checking on the names, but you can get around this easily. You see what I mean by switching some people out of the full price market into the cut-price market? Who loses? The airline does.

SKIMMING AND PRESTIGE PRICING

These two techniques are similar. Both operate at the top end of the market. One is designed to sell high quality at low financial risk; the other seeks to do the same but by using the price itself to promote the idea of status and prestige.

There is always a small group of people willing to pay high prices for what they want. They may have a very strong need for a particular product. They may have very substantial resources so that the price is of little concern within the context of the money they spend. How much does your company spend on its paper clips? Who knows? What's more, who cares? You don't. But the paper clip manufacturer does, and so does the stationery wholesaler from whom you buy your paper clips, when he buys in turn from the manufacturer.

A Volkswagen will get you to most places safely, securely and at economical miles per gallon. The operating cost will be very low. The price will be low. Why on earth should anyone pay anything more? Now have a look at the car driven by your company chairman. Is it a VW or something similar? No, it is not. His wife may have a VW while he drives a Jaguar or Mercedes, but that's only because we live in a chauvinistic society.

He needs to be seen in a prestige car. It is part of his self-image. And he will pay for that privilege. (Fierce arguments break out now from the Jaguar owners. "It's the comfort," they say; "I need to work in the car," they add. "With long drives you must arrive fresh," etc. Nonsense. The reason they have a Jaguar is because they want to be seen in a Jaguar.)

Now automobile manufacturers sell more economy cars than luxury cars. Indeed, in order to promote the sale of luxury cars, they sometimes reduce prices. But there is a demand at the top end of every market. And the price skimmers go for it. They do not sell in huge volume, but they do not need substantial manufacturing plants nor great overheads. They make money, and they sleep at nights. Their market sectors tend to be more stable in bad times than the major market sectors. They sell to people with money. Generally, they have less hassle about price than those who sell to people without money.

Ferrari sells relatively few cars worldwide. If they found that another make, say Porsche, was creeping up toward their price, they would be horrified. Immediately they would move for a price *increase*, in order to protect their reputation! That is the prestige pricing product for you. They must be at the top. Everything they do reeks of class and perfection. They don't sell many cars. But they make a lot of money on the cars they do sell.

That is a very comfortable way of business for a small specialist company without large resources. For a company that can produce brilliantly at the top-quality end that some people want, the skimming-price or the prestige-price system is recommended. But notice one proviso: The quality produced must be relevant to what some people want. It is not a question of producing what the technicians call "quality." It is not quality for its own sake. It is quality which is relevant to the performance which the buyer wants. And the quality for such producers must extend to everything they do. It must extend to their switchboard, the efficiency with which they handle correspondence, the truth of their sales story, and so on. That is the way to a successful and profitable life—not *the* most profitable life, because in terms of absolute cash profits, you need more sales volume. But it is a good life.

PENETRATION PRICE

Penetration pricing technique is used to undercut the market significantly and in such a way as to make it impossible for competitors to respond. As a result, there is a major increase in sales volume. It is an attractive idea in theory; but it is the route to disaster for most companies if they are forced into it.

To give some examples, the major airlines of the world are being dragged into an intercontinental price fight through the breakdown of International Air Transport Association price-fixing regulations. For 10 years, one of the world's leading airline opponents of air fare discounting has been Qantas. Yet by the early 1980s Qantas was applying to the Australian government to allow them to discount fares. In the end they were forced to copy. The Distillers company of Great Britain has long dominated the world supply of scotch. But with 45 malt distilleries in Scotland working half-time, Distillers introduced a new cut-price brand of whisky to be sold to small retail outlets.

None of the above is using true penetration pricing techniques. All of them are responding deliberately to pressures of the market and of competition. They are using promotional pricing methods.

The penetration pricing method was used successfully by Baron Bic, the ball point pen manufacturer, for example. When ball point pens were first introduced, they were sold as expensive gift items and were rather rare, with considerable personal prestige attached to ownership. Banks, however, refused to allow them to be used for signing checks in case the signatures wore off. Along came Baron Bic who built an enormous factory. He perceived ball point pens as a mass market product to be sold widely in thousands of outlets and at low prices. He took no notice of the existing market and of the existing prices. He sold them as cheap items, and build an enormous fortune as a result.

So, if you are thinking of a penetration price technique, then you must be brave. You must perceive that the market can be distorted for all time out of its present shape. You must perceive that a large number of new users will come to you and you will open up a substantial new market, previously untapped. The existing competition must be unable to compete with you on your price. You must have some technology available to you that is beyond the capacity of your competitors. And you must cut deep. Very deep. Don't even think in terms of 15% or 25%. You must think of 40% off the existing prices or even more. Maybe as much as 75% off.

Fortune favors the brave. When it doesn't, the brave are called stupid.

You can be like the Japanese. You look at a Mercedes and ask your technicians to produce the same overall performance, perhaps with some shading on the top speed. Then you produce your version for one third the price of the Mercedes. And you call it a Datsun. You do this with all your makes of car, in each price bracket. And you take over the world.

That is the penetration price technique. Have you the nerve for it?

Question: *Even if you have the nerve, can you use someone else's money to finance it? Just in case.*

SURVEYING THE MARKET

I wish there were a way in which this section could be more helpful to you—but most of the answers from market research are inadequate. The reason why companies do not use prices based upon what the market will bear is that there is no truly adequate way of measuring what the market will bear. You cannot ask 3,000 people in a survey what they think they will pay for a new type of toothbrush. They do not know the answers themselves until they are actually buying it.

In some industries there is enough competitive information published with great frequency that the volume sales of a product at any given price can be predicted with accuracy. In commodity trading, for example, all that is necessary is to study the market reports.

In consumer markets, specialized market information can sometimes be drawn from panel studies. If individual purchases of toothbrushes are measured by an panel over a period of time, it may be technically possible to identify how the market will respond to price promotions. A market test in one area may be used for predicting market reactions across the country.

In industrial markets the research techniques available are extremely limited. They are also costly and time consuming. The element of management judgment in setting market-related prices is extremely high in industrial marketing.

The best rule is to remember that the key factor at the end of the day will be judgment based upon experience of the market. Use every piece of evidence that can be gathered and that is reliable to assist in this judgment. Every time there is a price change, record the results. Measure the market and its various segments; compare the competitors' prices serving those segments.

In the United States and in Europe, many research companies have attempted to solve pricing questions with specialized market trial techniques or other direct research methods. The applications are very limited and the results are often rather abstract and uncertain. But do investigate the technical possibilities of using market research—a valid technique may exist in your particular market. But do not let your researchers become too excited about data based upon small samples. Forty respondents are not going to tell you how to price your industrial product with any degree of reliability—and it may cost you $7,000 to interview them if the product is in any way technical.

In consumer markets, try to avoid asking people about their future intentions, or their opinions about price. Better to conduct some kind of trial on an orderly basis and then observe their behavior. After that you can ask for their opinions.

Figure 5.3
Primary and secondary research sources

PRIMARY MARKET TRIAL	Trying out one or more prices in different areas/customers or applications. Sales and profit results are then compared.
Do	*Don't*
Use equal level of effort in each area.	Assume competitors will not notice.
Select comparable areas.	Imagine the results will be conclusive.
Select stable areas.	Imagine you can isolate nonprice factors from the results.
Run trial for long enough to evaluate results.	Sit in the office for results. Go and see what's happening for yourself.
MARKET SURVEY	Conducting face-to-face research with a statistically valid sample. There are enormous limitations to the use of this method for inquiring about buying intentions when related to projected prices.
Do	*Don't*
Ask questions related to beliefs about *other* companies, not the respondent's own company.	Use anyone other than a qualified market researcher to draw up the questionnaire.
Ask respondents to describe past action, not future intentions.	Use your own sales force for interviewing about opinions.
Ask price questions indirectly.	Imagine the results will be accurate; they'll give you an indication at best.

Primary and secondary research sources (continued)

STATISTICAL ANALYSIS OF PRICE/VOLUME RELATIONSHIPS	Compare quantities purchased at different times and at different prices, noting the effect of price changes on volume.

Do	*Don't*
Keep accurate records of volume at different prices.	Imagine that price is the only cause of a change in volume.
Compare actual results against plan immediately.	Attempt correlation analysis without expert help.
Note immediately nonprice factors that affect results.	Use this method for new ventures.
Use for existing, long-standing products.	Use this method with a long distributive chain. (Inventories will confuse data.)

SECONDARY

Competitive prices lists. (Use as reference points against which you compare your prices.)

Competitive advertising and promotional literature.

Customer reports about competition and requirements.
Sales force, supplier, and distributor data on a regular feedback system.

Trade journal announcements of price changes and articles about competitors.

Trade associations.

Annual and financial reports of competitors.

Government statistics for industry price averages.

Financial reports on companies and industries.

THE PRICE OF THE MARKET LEADER

If you want to have the biggest selling product on the market, then it helps if you have one of the first brands into the market. And it helps further if you concentrate upon offering sound quality backed by efficient marketing, confident selling and effective advertising. If you get those things right, then it will also help if you set your prices at a premium of about 7% over the market average. If you want to be number two or number three brand it will help if you set your prices just below the market leader, but about 5% above the average of all the prices in the market.

That way, you will sell the most volume and make more money than anyone else in the market. The table below shows the results of A. C. Neilsen data on this topic.

Neilsen is one of two companies in the world recognized as being the major research organizations for consumer products; their analysis is drawn from soundly based samples of consumer markets. Whether the same is true for industrial markets or for service organizations is not known. The percentages might be more or less—more in well differentiated product markets, less in commodities. But the general trend will almost certainly remain constant although it cannot be researched and proved.

> *Market leaders make the most money. On the average their price is better, their volume is greater and their unit costs are lower. They do not find it difficult to make more money.*

So remember, if you want to outsell everyone then get your price about 7% above the average. You will become brand leader provided that you follow the rest of the advice also. Remember, be one of the first into the market and help to build the market up from small beginnings; offer very sound quality and

	Figure 5.4
Market size *(100)*	Prices
42% All other brands	Varied: majority below average.
58% Top 3 brands average	Market leader price: 7% above average
	Next two brands prices: 5% above average

> ### Figure 5.5
> #### The eight biggest advantages of becoming market leader
>
> 1 Premium price over the average
> 2 Higher sales volume
> 3 Higher gross profit platform
> 4 Bigger advertising spend
> 5 More power over buyers
> 6 Less risk in bad times
> 7 More control over competition
> 8 More able to improve quality

good value for the money; sell effectively and with confidence on a mass market basis; and ensure that your advertising, your product development and your promotion are thoroughly effective. Back them with consistent and thorough research so that you know you are offering what people want.

Then you will be market leader. If you say it quickly, then it sounds easy.

SUMMARY

In any pricing system, people go around with ideas of fairness in their minds. In some cases, there is no other way than to use a judgment of what is proper in setting a price. But fairness is never far away from people's thoughts. "Look how much profit you are making on that item. Your prices are unfair."

Psychology also plays its part in pricing. Using pricing points appeals to buyer's psychology. Offering one item of the product *free* if they buy four items of the product has a greater impact than if a 20% discount is offered for the

> ### Figure 5.6
> #### Nine things you must do to become market leader
>
> 1 Be early into the market
> 2 Be dedicated to success
> 3 Develop unique aspects of product
> 4 Work for long-term profits
> 5 Concentrate upon efficiency
> 6 Be sensitized to the market
> 7 Compete fiercely
> 8 Keep costs under extreme pressure
> 9 Keep competitors under price/promotion pressure

whole five purchases. Getting through people's mental barriers and prejudices and expectations is part of the pricing game.

Competitive markets, with many suppliers chasing buyers and all offering rather similar services and qualities—that is the field for promotional discounting. An extra edge is given to the sales story if a discount argument is used. The discount itself can be sold instead of the basic price. "*Save* $50 *today*" in a men's shop window has a powerful impact on people's minds." It also stops them from thinking that the price that they will have to pay for the suit is $149 (the full price was $199). Promotional pricing is difficult to control. Don't get into it unless you must.

In markets involving fashion or taste, the demand is fickle. It is malleable and changeable. The quality is often in the eye of the beholder. (Just look at the poor quality of stitching and materials used in the high-priced boutique fashions, and compare the quality with that offered by an old-line department store. But boutique fashions still sell.) In the fashion markets, a high price is necessary—it may even be the high price that itself is the intangible idea being put across.

New products, entering new markets that have not seen the like before, generally use a skimming price technique. It allows the producers a profit at a low manufacturing level. It is their hedge against things going wrong. The risk is minimized. Practically all radically new products start by a price skimming technique. It is the competitors who bring the prices down as they copy their way into the market.

A penetration price technique is dangerous, but it can be successful provided that the manager knows exactly what he is doing. A company with massive resources can use it with comfort. But a good rule of thumb is this: If your proposed very low price in the market does not succeed in gaining you extra business, will the move seriously damage the rest of your business as a whole? If the answer is that you cannot afford to fail, then don't do it.

If you are the market leader, don't be afraid of a price that is higher than the average. Some competitors will be above you in price, but more will be below you. They have to drop their price below yours because their product cannot sell as well as yours. So don't be afraid of asking for your due price premium if yours is the biggest selling brand in the business.

*   *   *

Now go back to the questionnaire at the start of this chapter and complete it again.

Finding the Soft Areas of the Market | 6

Before reading this chapter, complete the answers to these questions in the spaces on the left-hand side. Then without looking at the answers, read the chapter. Finally, complete the answers again, making any changes you think fit. Score both sets of your answers. This tells you how much the chapter has affected your opinion. Scores are at the end of the book (p. 197).

COULD YOU BECOME A MILLIONAIRE?

Q.1   *You are an aspiring business millionaire but still at school. You work hard at your studies. What is your principal aim:*

(a) To do well at sports; (b) to pass your examinations with flying colors; (c) to become a management trainee; (d) to get a part-time job on weekends as well as to do your paper round; (e) to chase the girls; (f) to buy and sell secondhand comics, cassette tapes and recorders to your friends and neighbors?

Score   **Score**
_____   _____

            Before reading chapter.   *After reading chapter.*
_____   _____

Q.2   *Will you expect to make your millions out of:*

(a) Dealing in markets that are familiar to you; (b) dealing in many different kinds of markets, wherever profit opportunities exist; (c) dealing in familiar markets at first, then later going into unfamiliar ventures; (d) developing new markets from scratch; (e) going for small but high price market sectors with less competition?

Score   **Score**
_____   _____

            Before reading chapter.   *After reading chapter.*
_____   _____

Q.3   *As a budding millionaire you know that you will need money—preferably you want to use other people's money to finance your ideas. But if other people put up the money they will want a slice of the action. How can you avoid losing control:*

(a) By fast growth; (b) by going into ventures with a positive cash flow, i.e., you take the customers' money before you have to pay out to meet the bills; (c) by making substantial profits on a small capital base; (d) by using every

form of finance you can think of where they will not want equity, i.e., your creditors are kept waiting for payment, you borrow from your aunt, you use loans from the bank, you demand fast payment from customers, you borrow against insurance policies?

Score   **Score**
_____   _____

Before reading chapter.   *After reading chapter.*

_____   _____

Q.4
                                                                      Yes   No

(a) *You have made your millions out of selling the basic necessities of life in huge volume. Hundreds of stores carry your name. Would you use price promotions, offers and discounts extensively in your business?*

(b) *You have made your millions selling dreams. You are into entertainment, rock music, films and the leisure industry. Would you use price promotions, offers and discounts extensively in your business?*

(c) *You have made your millions out of the five-star hotel industry. All things being equal (politics, costs, etc.) would you set up your new hotel in Hong Kong where there are many five-star hotels already? (Your alternative site is in Lagos, Nigeria, where there are few.)*

Score   **Score**
_____   _____

Before reading chapter.   *After reading chapter.*

_____   _____

Q.5 *How good are your chances of becoming a millionaire?*

	Very unlikely	*Unlikely*	*Possible*	*Likely*	*Excellent*
(a) *You are a top manager with a multinational company*	1	2	3	4	5
(b) *You have a scientific background*	1	2	3	4	5
(c) *You are prepared to sacrifice everything, nearly, for your aim*	1	2	3	4	5
(d) *You are a woman*	1	2	3	4	5

(e)	*You have had two near miss financial crashes in the past*	*1*	*2*	*3*	*4*	*5*
(f)	*You are cynical, cold, callous, ruthless and manipulative*	*1*	*2*	*3*	*4*	*5*
(g)	*You are gracious, charming and kind, and you've made one million already*	*1*	*2*	*3*	*4*	*5*
(b)	*You have a very good idea of what people want, and the price they will pay for it*	*1*	*2*	*3*	*4 5*	

Score

___

Before reading chapter.   *After reading chapter.*

___

Score

___

___

Q.6   *You are in financial trouble and you need to buy into a new venture to help out your business. Which three of these would you look for:*

(a) A big exsisting market you can force your way into; (b) a product that will sell to people who have money to spend; (c) a product that is purchased very frequently, the customers all know it well and its competitors; (d) a product that can be sold direct to users and not through middlemen; (e) a product with a high fixed cost of manufacture making it expensive for competitors to copy; (f) a product that is distinctly different from its competitors, and better; (g) a market in which little loyalty exists for the present products?

Score

___

Before reading chapter.   *After reading chapter.*

___

Score

___

___

Scores
Becoming a millionaire is difficult; it is hard to get into the top bracket.

Above 30	You could make it. (Or are you one now?)
23–29	Don't give up hope.
14–22	Have you thought of joining the civil service?
Up to 14	Give up hope.

Finding the Soft Areas | 6
of the Market

There is a joke about the man who took out a woman who was so beautiful that he could hardly keep his eyes on the taximeter.

A psychologist would explain that, to such a man, the taxi fare was high on his Begrudging Index. The woman, on the other hand, would be low on his Begrudging Index, and with what a group of researchers have called a low "K" value. (P. Cooper, "Subjective economics: factors in a psychology of spending," Conference of the Market Research Society, 1964.)

THE BEGRUDGING INDEX AND THE K FACTOR

Put simply, there are some things which the average person does not like spending money on. He "begrudges" the expense. Taxi fares are high on his list (unless he can claim them as company expenses). But he, the average person, will spend money willingly on other things such as whiskey, entertainment, magazines— and girl friends. When he is on vacation, the average person will spend large sums on impulse items without begrudging the expense. Back at home he often would not buy the same item at all.

But another factor is at work also—the K factor. Within certain product ranges, the average customer is sensitive to differences in price, while in other product ranges he is less so. At higher prices, for example, only a small increase in quality is expected to be received for any given change in price (low K). But in the low price end of a market, for the same difference in price, a marked difference in quality is expected (high K).

Supposing you are a whiskey drinker—not heavy you understand, but whiskey is your favorite drink when it's time to relax. If you are near average, then you will have a favorite brand and you will know roughly how much it costs. You do not begrudge the expense—although you might grumble about it a bit from time to time. If, on some occasion, your favorite brand is not stocked, you might be asked to pay considerably more. In this case you will expect to receive a better quality whiskey. If you are asked to pay less than you pay usually, you will expect to receive a lower quality whiskey. Whiskey has a high K factor— changes in price are expected to be matched by changes in quality. Gasoline, on the other hand, has a low K factor—the prices at the pumps may be different in different parts of the country, but you expect the gasoline to be the same.

In general, whiskey drinkers will report afterward that a high price whiskey tasted "good" and a low price whiskey tasted "poor." Without wishing to be offensive to whiskey drinkers in any way, it must be pointed out that the most significant effect upon the average whiskey drinker's taste buds is the price

---

Figure 6.1
The elasticity of demand

It is difficult to calculate elasticity accurately because:

→ An organization cannot hold constant those items an economist assumes constant for analytical purposes (e.g., advertising, product differentiation).

→ Elasticity does not apply where products are not homogeneous, but differentiated.

→ Elasticity does not apply where any buyer or seller is large enough to influence demand.

→ Elasticity mistakenly assumes a company knows the shape of its demand curve (i.e., how much will be bought at each price).

---

difference! If you put a blindfold upon whiskey drinkers, they cannot select their own favorite brand from close competitors to any significant degree. And if you give them three sips of the *same* whiskey but tell them that one is cheap, one is expensive and one is normal, then they will report on the quality in line with the price. They will be able to identify bourbon from scotch, a rough from a smooth and a light from a dark whiskey, but within those categories, only one person in 200 has a palate that discriminates enough to enable close differences to be identified.

THE PRICE AS A QUALITY INDICATOR

For many products, the price itself is the most significant indicator of quality. If people understand that the quality can be taken for granted, then price promotions and discounts will help to move the product. Price promotions at the gasoline pump will always move more gasoline. They cannot always be guaranteed to move more whiskey.

Umbrellas have a low K factor. So does electricity. In general, if a low price is well promoted, or those products are put on special offers, then sales volume will increase.

THE VALUE OF MONEY

Money itself has a different value for different people. If you haven't got much of it, then spending $1 hurts you more than if you have a lot of it. It is a self-evident truth, but if you want to get more money for your products, sell them to the people who have got the money. Don't sell them to those without.

So to summarize, if you want to move into markets where it is easy to obtain a good price for what you sell, and where there is less threat of heavy price competition, look for the following opportunities.

Go for the products that make people feel better, that give them enjoyment, luxury or status. Don't go into products that satisfy basic needs. Sell dreams, not necessities. People do not begrudge the money so much.

Go for the markets where there are marked differences in quality offered. Preferably let your high quality differences be obvious to everyone, not hidden.

Figure 6.2
Elasticity: effect of price change on sales

	DEMAND IS		
	(More than 1) ELASTIC	*(=1)* UNITARY ELASTIC	*(Less than 1)* INELASTIC
If price is decreased			
Sales increase more than % decrease in price	X		
Sales increase proportionately to % decrease in price		X	
Sales increase less than % decrease in price			X
If price is raised and			
Sales decrease more than % increase in price	X		
Sales decrease proportionately to % increase in price		X	
Sales decrease less than % increase in price			X

You may have to highlight them artifically in some way. If your quality difference must remain intangible, then promote it heavily, and use a high price to "prove" the existence of your high quality.

Go for the top end of the market. The price elasticity of demand is low there by comparison to that of products sold at the bottom end of the market.

Find the people with money to spend and market your product to them. People without money may want your product badly, they may want you to sell it to them badly, they may have an obvious, glaring need for your product. But they will give you a hard time over your selling price. They will demand heavy discounts, because they haven't got money.

FREQUENCY OF PURCHASE

Yet another opportunity exists. Go for the products that people buy infrequently. If you set up a paint plant, then make small cans of specialized paints for specialized purposes; don't go for the high-volume market. The high-volume market will always be price sensitive. If you sell marine paint to a shipbuilding yard that specializes in oil tanker refits, you will sell a lot of paint but you will be skinned to your underwear. But if you sell small cans to ship chandlers, so that people can protect engine parts from saltwater corrosion, your price per gallon will be huge by comparison. But you will not sell so many gallons.

Evidence for this is widespread. In a supermarket study, 79% of shoppers recalled the price they paid for tea fairly accurately seven days afterwards. But flour prices were recalled accurately by only 36%. Tea has strong brand loyalty and is a frequent purchase. Flour purchases are less frequent and loyalty is weaker. So shoppers are more conscious of tea prices and price changes than they are of flour price changes.

PRODUCT LOYALTY

Loyalty is another factor that affects price sensitivity. Where a market can be secured loyally, customers are not so sensitive on price. For example, in scientific work in laboratories and in quality control work, there are many standard tests laid down and agreed upon. The standards concern the methods of testing and the materials to be used. A test to find whether a particular gas exists in the atmosphere may be run in the same way all over the world. Any alteration in the testing procedure or in the materials may affect the quality of result. Manufacturers of testing equipment would like the testing standard to be backed by law. What a way to secure your market, provided that you alone have laid down the standard!

> Marketing tip: *If you can get the law to insist that the customers buy your product, then your profits are assured and your price will be as high as the law will permit.*

As a consequence, manufacturers who supply laboratories are always searching for products that can be specified at the outset in the first trials. They know

that from then on, once the product has been adopted, the customer will be
"loyal." And one of the effects of that is that they can subsequently obtain a
very high price for the product. The most extreme example would be a life-
support drug without which a patient would die. The only constraining factor
on the price will be the morality of the supplier. In theory, he could charge up
to whatever the patient can afford. In practice, he does not charge so much—
many drug companies lose heavily on the life-support products, particularly as
the product line begins to age and the sales fall because new techniques have
overtaken them.

INDUSTRIAL INERTIA

Another word for loyalty could be inertia. Inertia is a characteristic of a great
deal of industrial purchasing. If you sell steel, the chances are that you will hold
your customer for an average of 11 years. In that time, you will have many
arguments with him about your price. Occasionally, he may threaten to bring
in a cheaper supplier. Sometimes he may even give a trial to a competitor of
yours. But the evidence is that, as long as you are reasonably competitive on
price, the customer will stick by you loyally. In all that time, he could probably
buy a little cheaper from someone else. He could also save money by shopping
around in the best market. But industrial companies are generally inert—it is
too much trouble to keep changing suppliers. It is too much of a risk to interrupt
their production process with a different material, even if the trial results are
good. So they live loyally with their existing suppliers for many long years.

Technical salesmen may be very successful in obtaining trials for their products
within industrial organizations. They put in free samples of the products, and
the technical staff evaluates them. Often the customers report that the trials are

---

Figure 6.3
How buyers assess materials

	Materials a small part of buyer's costs	**Materials a large part of buyer's costs**	
High risk to buyer	Quality conscious – less sensitive to price	Quality conscious – negotiated prices between competitors	*Technical involvement strong*
Low risk to buyer	Price conscious – routine competitive quotes	Price conscious – open to tenders	*Purchasing department involvement strong*

successful and that they had good results. The price might be competitive. Perhaps the customer can lower his costs as a result. The industrial salesman waits for the order. And waits. And waits. The customer has found it to be too much of a risk to switch over. Buying inertia has won again.

Advice on industrial selling: *Never press a man to a decision if he has only the power to say no. Go behind him to the man who can say yes. Many industrial buyers can only say no.*

Materials are usually the biggest single item of expense in a manufacturer's costs. Any change in the material cost has direct, immediate and punching impact upon the customer's profits. Yet the relationships between materials suppliers and their customers are among the most stable to be found in industry.

Where the products involve less risk of a wrong decision, the issue might turn more on price. Price wars can be set up by the buyers of those items under conditions of short demand.

When the products are bought by an individual buyer infrequently, the price arguments will not be so strong. But the more "expert" the buyer, the more he will concentrate upon price issues, taking quality features for granted.

PRICE AND THE PRODUCT LIFE CYCLE

Products become more sensitive to price when they are well established and everyone is used to them, in comparison to the time when they were new and exciting.

When a radical new product idea hits the market, it appeals usually to a small, specialized group of people. Such buyers are concerned more about the performance of the product and its reliability than they are about its price. They want to be reassured that the product will work, and that their money will not be wasted. Indeed, a high initial price may help to provide them with that very satisfaction—and it will also have the advantage of increasing the "rarity" value of the new product.

Later, as the market becomes used to the idea, new competitors enter the market. Usually they price down their product against the original brand so that price does not become a handicap to their sales. By this time buyers are more confident of their ability to purchase well and that, combined with an emphasis upon price promotion by the incoming new suppliers, makes everyone more price conscious.

The market continues its inexorable swing towards saturation, and as it does so, a wide variety of types of the basic product are introduced.

The market becomes segmented, and as a result, it becomes mature. There is an even heavier emphasis upon price competition, particularly where a quality product is not easily differentiated against the rest.

DISTRIBUTORS' MARGINS

Distributors, whether wholesalers or retailers, are always concerned with price—

Figure 6.4
Variables change with the product life cycle

Marketing Emphasis	Product quality	Adver-tising selling	Product develop-ment	Sales promotion	Pricing moves	Market segmenta-tion	Market develop-ment	Pricing moves	Cost control
Management Style	Venture management				Integrated management		Cash management		

not so much in terms of the actual unit price itself but with the percentage margin they can make as their profit when calculated against the likely sales volume. Any study of distribution will show that the volume-selling products provide them with a smaller percentge margin than the slower-selling lines. Also, the products with very high resale prices offer distributors a lower percentage margin than those with a lower price. A fast-selling product like bacon might give a retailer about 15–17% margin. That's about the same margin a car dealer would get for his products, which sell slowly by comparison but at high prices.

The distributor is in a peculiar situation as regards quality. Provided that the product works satisfactorily, and that he can sell it easily and service it easily, he is not himself worried principally about product quality. But he might be more concerned with the service he obtains from the supplier. He will be very concerned with the wholesale price margin and sales volume potential.

The end user is concerned principally with quality—those other factors of importance to the distributor are not important to the end user. The user may not be price sensitive at all. But the distributor will always be price sensitive in any sector of the market. And he has a predisposition to believe that his final customer is more price sensitive than he really is.

Few company purchasing officers really care how much they spend on paper staplers. Most of them would have to search through their records to find out how much they do pay. But the stationery wholesaler knows how much he pays and he knows how much the company pays. He knows his margin very well. Just because the industrial user of staplers does not care about the price, it does not stop the staplers supplier's being squeezed hard on his prices. He is squeezed by the wholesaler.

SUMMARY

From the foregoing, we can draw some strategic conclusions. First, some people do not worry too much about the price—they want quality. Find those people and work on them—let them pull the product through the professional buyers. Advertise to them, promote to them, keep the educational pressure going at them. Make yourself strong with those people, and you will weaken the position of those who can give you a hard time on price.

If you are selling to industry, then go behind the purchasing officer. Go to the technical staff. Go to general management. Go to the people who will be most affected by using the product—those are the people who care more about quality and less about price. If you reach only the company purchasing officer, you will be playing into his hands. If you leave him to deal with the people behind him, he will not do so as well as you can, and he will come back to pricing and discount arguments. Even if you offer the lowest priced product in the market, someone behind the purchasing man must be convinced that the quality is good enough. Find him. And sell him the quality—not the price.

If you are in consumer products, then you must make yourself powerful with the only one who matters in the long run—the consumer. You must advertise, you must make him want what you offer because of its distinctive qualities. The consumer will then pull the product through the distribution chain for you. The stronger your brand loyalty, the weaker the position of the middleman. The middleman, the wholesaler and the retailer will always give you a hard time on price. He will still argue for bigger discounts for himself. He will still want better margins, improved terms. He will still threaten to stop taking your product if you don't meet his requirements. But if your consumer brand loyalty is strong, it will be an empty threat. He must have your product in stock if his customers demand it. Whatever the price.

But if you are weak in the market, if you have no strong connection with the end users, if no one knows your brand name, if you sell to the retailers under their name alone—then they can squeeze you on price. And squeeze you they will—to the limit of what they believe you can afford. They might not squeeze you so hard that they will put you out of business—for how does that suit them? But they can squeeze you so that you don't make much money. Who will make the money instead? They will.

The second strategic point concerns product differences. Some products are very sensitive to price differences. Customarily those are the products that are undifferentiated from others, without distinctive merit or attraction. But there are other products and services for which people dislike paying. Often, they are the products supplied by the monopolist—if people must have the product and there is only one source from which to buy it, they feel themselves to be in a weak position. With such products, promotion on price will often be helpful. Such products are often the essential things of life—food, household goods, electricity, fuel.

But the lighter things of life, those that we enjoy, things that concern fashion or taste, and those that enhance our status—such products and services are much less sensitive to pricing arguments. Price promotions here will not help— well, not so much as with the necessities, anyway.

Finally, some people in the market have a lot more money than others. Products that sell at the bottom end of the market usually are sought out by one of three different kinds of customer. First, there is the customer who would like to buy better quality but who cannot afford it—he shops toward the floor price. Then there is the "expert" buyer, the one who is very confident of his own ability to spot the weaknesses and who has bought often enough before to be able to know that he can get what he wants. He shops toward the floor price, and concentrates upon pricing arguments. The expert buyer is very difficult to handle. Finally, there is the buyer who is not basically interested in the product at all, but must buy it for some reason. He will tend to buy it cheaply if he can, because he does not really care about it.

Such people all shop toward the floor price in any market segment. Avoid them; they are difficult to deal with. Go to the others who are interested in quality. You will have fewer arguments about price.

Old Chinese sellers' saying: *It is much easier to get money from people who have it than it is from people who do not.*

*   *   *

Now go back to the questionnaire at the start of this chapter and complete it again.

Competitor-related Pricing Systems

Before reading the chapter, complete the answers to these questions in the spaces on the left-hand side. Then without looking at the answers, read the chapter. Finally, complete the answers again, making any changes you think fit. Score both sets of your answers. This tells you how much the chapter has affected your opinion. Scores are at the end of the book (p. 198).

HOW GOOD WOULD YOU BE AS AN ENTREPRENEUR?

Q.1 *You have been a top manager with a multinational company, but you realize that you'll never make any real money if you work for just a salary. So you decide to take your courage in both hands and set up on your own account with the help of an inheritance. You know a lot about sailing, so you decide that boat building will be the vehicle for your success. You want to make money (quite difficult to do in the boating industry, but not impossible) and you know from experience that it pays to exert control over your market.*
    Which of the following kinds of boats would you consider building:

(a) Big individual boats built to custom order; (b) everyday dinghies with a mass market appeal; (c) a racing boat by a top international designer, exclusive to you; (d) all kinds of boats for your local area market?

Score   **Score**

———   ———

                 Before reading chapter.   *After reading chapter.*

———

Q.2 *You decide to build an exclusive one-design class boat, with a high racing performance. This approach means that the boats are standardized to produce and to fit out, and it minimizes the production cost. Your boat will appeal to the racing dinghy sailor who wants to try small-boat offshore racing. How will you price your boat by comparison with the competition?*

(a) Offer a discount price against their equivalent boat; (b) go for price leadership just above the middle of the market; (c) go for big market share with a very low price; (d) negotiate price with individual buyers?

Score   **Score**

———   ———

                 Before reading chapter.   *After reading chapter.*

———

Q.3 *You go for price leadership, but you now have to control the market as best*

*you can. Two sailmakers want to produce sails for your boat, which is begin-
ning to win good racing events and is getting excellent reports in yachting
magazines. You can't stop anyone from making sails for your boat but you
can yourself buy and recommend specific makers. What terms do you insist
on? Racing boat owners buy new sails every other season, so there is a con-
tinuing "after market."*

*(a) Exclusive selling rights through you alone by one maker; (b) let them
compete with each other openly for the market, shaving off a percentage
margin to you; (c) your business is building boats; selling sails is very iffy
and not worth the effort. Let all the sailmakers look after it themselves; all
are encouraged to make sails for your boats; (d) license two of them, but on
condition that the selling prices are all agreed upon between you and them;
you will receive a discount on the sails you buy for your new boats, and in
addition both you and they will sell to existing owners.*

Score   **Score**
———   ———

            Before reading chapter.   *After reading chapter.*
———

Q.4   *One way to attract boat owners is to insure that the secondhand value of
their craft remains high. But you cannot influence that market so easily.
You can only influence it mildly, if at all. Boat selling prices are chaotic;
few people know values. Do you:*

*(a) Advise all your boat owners regularly in a newsletter about the prices at
which they should sell secondhand boats—a kind of "price guide"; (b) do
this, but also get the class association secretary to circulate this guide to owners
who appear to be advertising their boats at too low a price; (c) leave the
secondhand market to look after itself; the lower the prices, the more popular
the class will become in general, you believe; (d) insist on all boats being sold
back to you, in the original contract?*

Score   **Score**
———   ———

            Before reading chapter.   *After reading chapter.*
———

Q.5   *A lot of boat owners like to have a hand in making their own boats. It is
too big a market segment for you to ignore, and you cannot control the
purchase of every fitting on every boat. In addition to selling completely
finished boats, do you:*

*(a) Sell plans for building the boat, from scratch; (b) sell the molded hull
and decking, leaving owners to do the rest while offering them kits of parts;
(c) make practically everything yourself, leaving the owners to just finish off*

if they want to, putting in the lining in the cabin and so on, with you supplying all the parts; (d) ditto, but in addition have the boat rated for offshore racing by the Yachting Association, which ties down every little specification tight? Without a rating certificate, the boat will not be allowed to compete in important events with a sensible handicap.

Score   **Score**

———   ———

Before reading chapter.   *After reading chapter.*

———   ———

In all of the questions above there are important lessons in competitive market influence. The market as a whole is fragmented and chaotic. A company must emerge from this mess. Sensible business planning is the only way—and it is never far removed from pricing policy and strategy.

Scores

Above 22	You must be in the boat business.
18–21	You could get into the boat business
12–18	Don't go into the boat business.
11 or less	Don't go into any business.

Competitor-related Pricing Systems

The trouble with competition is that you can't trust it. Whereas you yourself are a model of truth, honesty and reliability, your competitor does not fight fair. When you give your word, your word holds. If only your rivals would stick to the agreements you make with them.

Throughout the centuries, men have collaborated to rig the market. In Athens, at the time of Plato, politicians were arguing that a group of grain merchants should be put to death for fixing prices. The record exists today of the speech in the court: "It is necessary, gentlemen of the jury," the speaker urged, "to chastise them not only for the sake of the past, but also as an example for the future. If you act wisely, you will buy grain cheaper, otherwise dearer." An appeal to self-interest has always provided a closing opportunity for the salesman.

In June, 1981, a secret price-fixing agreement between six companies who supply British homes with gas-fired boilers was banned. They were not six tiny engineering companies. They were major national concerns with quotations on the stock exchange—household names, in fact.

In the City of London in the year 1199, an attempt was made to control the wholesale and retail price of wine in the City. The cartel was difficult to enforce and eventually failed.

In the early 1980s, President Houphouet Boigny of the Ivory Coast was causing some disquiet to his competitors. His competitors believed that the price of cocoa on the world market was too low, and they sought an agreement among themselves that it should be raised. Unfortunately, the Ivory Coast supplies 22% of the world market, and Boigny does not join clubs set up by his competitors. So they were angry with him.

The consumer countries, the EEC and the United States, would not join in that happy little cocoa agreement either, but it did not matter much. In May, cocoa prices were down to the lowest for five years. In June, the rest of the countries went ahead with their cocoa price pact, leaving out the Ivory Coast. In July the cocoa price for September futures was up more than 12%.

In South Africa, diamond mine owners had a bad time around the end of the last century. The diamond buyers formed a cartel and squeezed all the mine owners to the limit. Many owners lost all they had. One man came along and bought up all the mines for a pittance. Having secured the source of production, he then took diamonds off the market. The buyers pleaded with him to sell to them. They had customers to service. The more they pleaded, the more he broke them, one by one. In the end he took over the buying ring as well as the source of production. And so the great diamond trading company of the world, which today stabilizes and controls the mining, the processing and cutting, and the wholesale distribution and prices of 85% of the world's diamonds, the De Beers company, was formed. The man's name? Cecil Rhodes. He went on to found the country which carried his name for over 90 years.

Rings, cartels, market fixers? You'll never get rid of them. They recur through history a thousand times. At the same time this book was written, four antique dealers were banned from auctions for being caught in a buying ring. Has this stopped such rings at auctions? No. It has caused the ringers to become more careful about being caught. The OPEC countries such as Nigeria, Venezuela, Iraq, and Libya were all pleading with Saudi Arabia to stop producing so much oil. With a glut on the world market, the prices were low. Until they could stop their competitor from producing too much, they could not raise their prices again.

That's the trouble with competition. You can't trust it.

THE PRICE LEADER

Most markets are divided into segments of varying kinds. Some segments offer high quality and high levels of service, and take high prices. Others offer as little as they can and price it low. There are others in between. There are distinct kinds of buyers involved for each segment. In each market sector, you will find a "price leader." This is the company in the market that is used by its competitors as a yardstick for comparison. Commonly, he is the market leader and has the biggest selling product in that segment of the market, but that is not always necessarily so. He is the one who tends to make the first move on prices, up or down, and his competitors tend to follow. He is often the one who behaves very aggressively towards his own competitors if he thinks they are misbehaving. I can remember when I was a young marketing manager in a food company, being telephoned regularly by the marketing director of a big company competitor who was complaining that this salesmen were reporting to him that our prices in some outlets were too low. Would I oblige him by putting them up?

This was an unusual situation and outside my experience at the time, but generally we went along. Later the competitor's marketing director was promoted to another company and the phone calls stopped. Another fierce competitor started attacking their accounts directly and using price discounts. The big company failed to respond. They lost their price leadership, because others started looking toward the newcomer as their yardstick on price. Within three years they had lost their overall market leadership. In later years I came to regard the marketing director's telephone calls as being a very important aspect of his psychological domination of the market. If he were there today, they might still be market leader.

Remember, when your competitor telephones you, he is more concerned with you helping him than he is with helping you.

If you use competitive pricing as your principal technique, then pick the price leader in your segment. If you offer a discernible product difference, a distinct improvement that the market definitely wants (not what you think it should want), and you can sell that difference hard, take a premium price a shade over your chosen competitor. Don't pick all the competitors—just pick the key one and go for him, on his weakness in product or on service performance.

If you offer nothing over your competition, but what you offer is comparable to what he offers, then underprice him by between 10% and 15%. It must be that size of discount against him if you don't offer any advantage. If you yourself are the price leader, then maintain your psychological domination over your competitors using a little reward and punishment. Be nice to them when they do something you like or behave the way you want them to behave. Turn nasty when they do not behave properly. If you are going to turn nasty, then turn very nasty indeed, so they won't do it again. Otherwise they'll begin to enjoy setting you up.

MARKET SHARE PRICING

This is very similar to the penetration price technique with very deep discounting. Remember that competitors will not sit back and let their sales go without a fight, and some of them will fight dirty. You are going to start a price war— the buyers will see to that. "Sorry, can't do business today," they smile. "Just had a good offer in from a rival. You can have the business, but you'll have to beat their price." And that is the way the price war starts.

Don't try market-share pricing in a high technology market—the market is more price sensitive toward the bottom end with "me-too" products. A twin segment strategy can be quite useful for a market share pricing technique. This involves securing your profits by your operations in the high price, high value sector of the market, but dumping out your grade B product or your second brand to keep the competition down. One specialist paper company has 90% share of the British market, where it keeps its prices very high. Similarly, it does the same in the United States, South Africa and Australia where its share is high. It does not sell in Germany where there is a big rival company, also high priced; it does not speak to the German company ever, but the feeling is that while it does not sell in the German market, then perhaps the Germans will not sell in the British market.

But the paper company drops its prices down low in Singapore, Hong Kong and Japan, right down toward the cost of production. There it wants to keep down a Japanese competitor on his home ground. The Japanese company has a high share of its own market and the paper company keeps the attention concentrated upon the fight there, hoping that the Japanese company will not break out into world markets. Of course, that's not fighting dirty.

That is honest, healthy, vigorous competition! Low prices, going for market share, can be very unprofitable unless you have substantial resources tucked up your sleeve.

DISCOUNT PRICING

This is different from promotional pricing in that the discounts are used as a
way of life. The technique is to set an artificially high price, and then to discount
off it. Every time you see a classified ad in the paper that adds the words "or
best offer" after the price, you are in the hands of a discounter whether he
knows it or not. Everyone knows the advertised price is not real, and bargaining
commences. Discount prices can be formally published as a series of offers for
a given time or for a given quantity.

Discounts might not be published, however. In which case, if the buyer does
not ask, then he does not get. The professional buyer handles his interviews
with care. He pulls in two or three companies for quotations and finds out
what he can get from each of them. Then he pulls in his chosen company and
squeezes it to give all the concessions the others have offered to him. So the
bargaining hassle begins.

Everyone knows that car dealers will reduce the price of a secondhand car.
But the buyer has to negotiate it. The dealer will give away as little as he can.
But he will still discount if asked. Luckily for the salesman, not every car buyer
has the courage to ask.

Advice on discount pricing: Don't publish discounts if you can avoid it. You
will do better if you negotiate them individually. Secondly, if you are discounting, then vary the terms a lot. Put a time limit on every deal and then renegotiate
it. Whatever you do, don't let your discounts become rooted in the structure
of your price list, otherwise you will give away money for nothing. If you must
do this, because everyone else does it, then set the prices higher than usual and

Figure 7.1
How does industry offer its discounts?

By means of a formally published discount
structure in the price list   49%

By means of informal discretionary discounts that
are negotiated   51%

Companies that formally publish their discounts also use a two-tier discount
structure by negotiating special deals, particularly with special classes of
customer, such as large key accounts.

Source: *How British Industry Prices*, Industrial Market Research, 1975

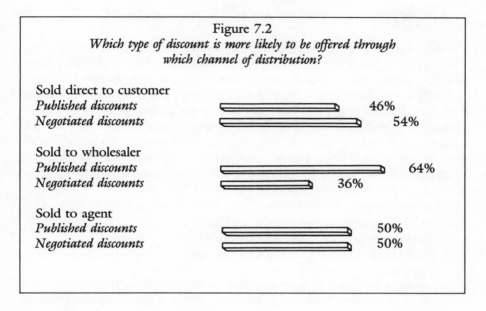

Figure 7.2
Which type of discount is more likely to be offered through which channel of distribution?

Sold direct to customer
Published discounts 46%
Negotiated discounts 54%

Sold to wholesaler
Published discounts 64%
Negotiated discounts 36%

Sold to agent
Published discounts 50%
Negotiated discounts 50%

show even bigger discounts. But generally keep the situation as flexible for yourself as possible.

NEGOTIATED PRICES

Here we have the full range of maneuver at work. Each party starts in a situation of some uncertainty about the other, which gradually becomes clarified. Each party is conscious of its alternatives—the buyer seeks to maintain competition for his business for as long as possible and will use that leverage in discussion. The seller uses the uniqueness of his proposition and its relevance to the buyer's situation in order to back his demands for price. The buyer raises price as soon as he can in the discussion—sometimes demands it in writing before discussion. The seller seeks to announce his price as late as possible in the discussion, once the buyer's excitement has been aroused. The buyer will seek to get as many extras as possible included in the overall price. The seller will seek to unbundle the package and price each of his items separately. The buyer will seek to leave his requirements on some matters open until after the agreement has been signed, so he can add them in at no cost later. The seller will seek to have some part of the agreement left open-ended, so that he can add bits and pieces to his prices later.

All human life is there—there is a rich variety of stratagems covering so many aspects of human behavior. Some deals are quick, some deals are slow. The way the first deal's price is set up conditions the mood and behavior in subsequent deals.

COMPETITIVE PRICING IN A DECLINING MARKET

Before rushing into price change action, you must determine the causes of the falling sales. If, for example, your product, style or service is suffering from deficiencies then you will rarely correct them with a price reduction.

Perhaps your customers' demand has fallen and the industry is in recession. A price reduction may help, but only if it is passed on to their customers. Perhaps your trade is overstocked, in which case the problem will resolve itself once the inventories are cleared. Perhaps the sales of a major product to which your own product is related have fallen. A price reduction will not help this situation. The market may be saturated and may be turning to alternative technologies. A price reduction will not help there either. The principal questions to ask in a declining sales situation, when pricing action is contemplated, are:

—What is the long-run implication of a price change?
—Would it be better to offer a larger but temporary discount?
—Would you solve the problem and buy some time if you just negotiated temporary larger discounts to the big customers?
—Would it be better to meet all the competitive price reductions to your distributors—but how could you stop a discount battle breaking out?
—Would it be better to lose some volume and market share in the short term rather than to take price cuts across the board?

Figure 7.3
Pricing in a declining market

SEVEN THINGS NOT TO DO

Confuse rumors with reality. Beware price wars started by customers.

Confuse sales decreases with market share decreases.

Blame price alone for sales decline.

Concentrate on some prices to exclusion of others.

Wait for the crisis to resolve itself.

Drop prices before it is necessary.

Believe that you offer the right price for all time.

Figure 7.4
What are discounts offered for?

Answers add up to more than 100% because companies often offer discounts on a variety of different bases.

Quantity bought per order ⊏══════⊐ 46%

Quantity bought over a period ⊏═════⊐ 39%
of time

A special category of customer ⊏════════⊐ 57%

For cash or settlement ⊏═════⊐ 33%

This result reflects the power of large customers to influence the discounts they are offered. By "category of customer" is meant very large accounts usually.

HOW TO STOP A DISCOUNT BATTLE

This is not going to be easy for you. Not unless you have 80% share of the market or more, in which case you can just snap at the competition, draw a little blood and your problem is finished. The post office never has trouble with its prices, does it? The problem is that for every company that has 80% share of its market, there are thousands that have less, much less. So you will be one of those companies. If you are lucky, you might have 20% share, with two other companies with about 20% share each. First of all, stop them from cutting up each other, and you. That is vital. If only two of you will agree, then between you you'll have to go hard for the third one until he conforms. The three of you then go together for the others in the market, starting with each market segment leader or area market leader. Ask them, nicely, to stop it, and be able to prove your knowledge of their prices. In a discount battle, when things have got out of hand, then management itself often does not know what net prices its salesmen have been offering. Some of them are not too pleased when they find out.

If they will not conform the nice way, then you must go for them the nasty way. You pick off their key accounts; you go in and make such huge offers that the customers cannot refuse. You must do this even if you lose money on the deal—even below the costs of production if you have to. Remember, you are exerting your psychological power. In the course of thumping them hard, you are going to get hurt yourself.

If you want to frighten them off, you won't do it if you just slap their wrists. You will have to go for the jugular.

And remember, all this time, that you must hold in the goodwill and support of your two other big competitors in this campaign. Unless they see that they too must get a little hurt here and there, but that it is in everyone's interest to stop the discount battle spreading to all out war, then you've had it.

As you can see, your chances of stopping a heavy discount battle are remote, even if you are fairly sizeable in the market. Only major companies, with massive resources prepared to take substantial short-term losses, can do it.

Try to limit the damage the discount battle does to you. First, secure your basic business with your principal customers. Tighten up on the personal service, improve the efficiency, and make it difficult for competitors to break in. Don't snatch at every stray piece of business. Use every device you can think of as an alternative to price cutting. At the time of writing it is very difficult to sell new cars. The market has dropped by 15% and there are thousands of car workers being laid off. Cut prices are being offered everywhere. One company competes on price, but it is also offering free driving lessons—an attempt to increase sales to first time buyers and driving schools. It's an intelligent way of competing on price.

Limit the discount battle to some markets, some customers if you can. Whenever there is a glut of gasoline and a shortage of demand, then a discount battle breaks out among gasoline stations. The oil companies are forced to support their dealers' price cuts; otherwise the big dealers will not renew their contracts with the company. So what the companies do is to gradually move their "support" discounts around the market. One area will enjoy large rebates to help them price cut this month, but next month the rebates will move to another area. In this way, the effect of the damage to the companies is limited.

Centralize your pricing decisions and do not delegate much discount discretion down the line to the salesmen. They won't like it; but you just do it. You and only you should have the power to vary the price.

IT WON'T SOLVE THE PROBLEM

If you really want to know the correct answer to a discount battle, it is this. Make sure that what you offer is unique, that no one else can offer it. Make sure that that unique aspect is what some of the customers want. Make sure you sell it effectively, preferably in the upper part of the market on price. Make sure that you produce consistently reliable quality. And make sure that your service is first class. Don't let your product get out of date, technically.

I won't promise that as a result you will never get into a discount battle. But you will win through hardly noticing, while the others are scrabbling for the bits.

TENDERING

One of the most difficult problems facing the manager will be the price at which to submit a tender. When several companies offer very similar products or services, then a large customer, typically a local government department, may ask several firms to bid for the contract.

Companies usually seek to find out all they can about the expectations of the customer before submitting their bids, but it is in the nature of things that customers are very reluctant to give out information about competitors' bids or other factors involved. Once the specification has been drawn up and offered to the market, then it is too late for a supplier to do much about it. On the other hand, it has been known often enough in the past for news of a forth-coming tender to be leaked to suppliers well in advance. Suppliers' technical experts then have a vested interest in getting behind the purchasing department to the people who will be concerned with drawing up the specification. If these people can be influenced by technical arguments to draw up the specification in such a way that very few companies—perhaps only one company—can meet it, then the bid can go in at full price in the clear knowledge that it is the only one which can be accepted. The opportunity to do this may be limited, but it may be worth trying where possible.

Equally, there may be other small advantages that can be promoted. For example, it is not always the lowest tender that is accepted. If two tenders are close to each other and one of them comes from within the local area, the local firm will usually get the contract. If one company can offer a reciprocal trading arrangement with the large customer, that will give him an edge.

If, in handling the contract, a supplier can show that he will use local labor, which will help the employment situation in an area, that may give him an edge on price. Look at the features of your proposition that lie outside the specification itself and promote them.

SUMMARY

Having looked at what the market will bear, you now have to look at what you offer and compare it to what the competition offers. Then you must compare competitive prices.

Throughout history, men have tried to control their competitors' selling prices, or control the prices that rival buyers are willing to pay. Sometimes their efforts have been backed by the force of law. Collusion may work, but its effects are usually distorted in some way. Price rigging systems break down when one of the competitors is too weak, or becomes greedy, or when there is a lack of trust between competitors. If the market is depressed the sellers' price rings break down.

But controlling and shaping the market price should be an important aspect of every company's business plan—it is mandatory for a market-leading product that is intended to remain market leader.

It is important for a company to examine with precision where it is strong against competition—and where competition is stronger. The differences need to be priced in terms of what the market will pay. Compare yourself to the market leader in your segment, but also have a look at the kind of customers you sell to. The different customer outlets may be your strength—or they may be the very reason why your prices are low.

Don't go for market share pricing unless you really know what you are doing. Don't do it just when you are in trouble and all other simple solutions have failed. Don't do it if your competitors are able to copy you. You will have started a price war, in which everyone loses.

On big deals, particularly those involving complex technical discussions, negotiate prices individually. And be careful who does the negotiation on your behalf—there is a very high level of skill involved, and there is no substitute for experience.

Don't publish your discounts, if you can avoid it; keep them on a short rein, so they can be renegotiated or renewed from time to time. Then, if you give a discount to someone, you can make sure they give something back to you in exchange. Otherwise they'll take the discount and give you nothing back.

Your chances of stopping a discount battle by yourself are next to nil, unless you have the resources of Fort Knox. So if you can't stop it, don't start it. You may rue the day if you do. Compete on anything but price if you can; deal with customers who have money, and teach your salesmen how to handle buyers who skin you. Cut back your costs, and trim your organization tight, but don't cut down on customer service. Actively improve customer service, then sell it hard. That will be your competitor's weakness.

*   *   *

Now go back to the start of the chapter and complete the questionnaire again.

Handling Fierce Price Competition | 8

IS YOUR MARKETING DIRECTOR A WARMONGER?

Q.1 *Consider these statements and quickly circle the number that best represents the firmness of his position on it.*

	Very true of him	Usually true of him	No feelings either way	Usually untrue of him	Very untrue of him
If a competitor is lower he wants to get under their price	5	4	3	2	1
He would like to talk to competitors about equalizing prices	1	2	3	4	5
He would start a discount battle any time; he believes the first one in wins	5	4	3	2	1
Before quoting a special price he always asks: Why?	1	2	3	4	5
He is even prepared to lose some deals on price	1	2	3	4	5
He always keeps it simple if he can. "Cut 10%" is the way to do it	5	4	3	2	1
He tries not to publish his discounts, and would rather negotiate them individually	1	2	3	4	5
As the chief, he always offers bigger discounts than he allows his men to offer	5	4	3	2	1
He believes that most people will jump at a 10% discount	5	4	3	2	1
He believes that people who start savage price wars often regret it	1	2	3	4	5

See p. 199 for comments.

Handling Fierce Price Competition | 8

In the old days, it was possible to start a war against another nation and hope to win it. You might be a little battered or bruised, but you could hope, with luck, to break the enemy's will to initiate war or to continue fighting once the war had started.

But the nuclear age has changed all that. The entire theory of nuclear defense is based on the idea that no one will start a war because no one can win. Both sides will be devastated.

Now the nuclear defense idea is marvellous if you have only a few people with the weapons. The governments can establish a hot line between each other. The penalties for not agreeing to stop before the war starts are obvious and can be established quickly between the heads of half a dozen governments.

Whenever power is concentrated within a few hands, then control can be exercised. The same is true in industry. Where a few suppliers appear to dominate the market to a great extent, then people are suspicious of their motives and of their behavior. Socialist economists have always been attracted to the examination of the seven sisters, the major oil companies in the world, because of their apparent ability to control the market between them. Indeed, Standard Oil of New Jersey was set up and run by Rockefeller on the basis of controlling the market, making it impossible for the independent oil-well producer to sell outside his organization. The big oil companies controlled the market until the day we began to run short of oil, which, at last, to the practical possibility of a successful producers' cartel, called OPEC.

Prices of gasoline move upward almost in unison. But the oil companies do fight each other with discounts, allowances and rebates. They are not large, but they are enough to keep the market buoyant and competitive. A *real* price war among the seven sisters oil companies is absolutely unthinkable. A real price war is a knock-down, drawn-out killer struggle which ends up with someone going to the wall. The oil giants will not do that to each other.

When the nuclear weapons are dispersed among many nations, the real trouble starts. One nation will not accept the notion that it will destroy itself if it wages war; another may not care; yet another may be led by a madman; and another nation may build up such hatred of an enemy that it will be blind to the consequences of launching a nuclear attack.

Similarly, a fragmented market in a recession becomes a battleground for a real price war. During the war some companies will expire. They will experience death by a thousand price cuts.

Capacitors are small electronic components. A defense contract will call for hundreds of thousands of them. Your home video equipment will need far fewer. Countless millions of them are used in the aerospace industry. Two big American companies have large slices of the world market; those companies have huge resources of money and skill, enough you would think to fight off anyone. But they are being overwhelmed by the hordes from the Far East.

A contract for capacitors may be placed, and after a tough struggle the buyer agrees to pay 20¢ per capacitor. That allows the supplier very little profit, but he is relieved to get the order. Next week, the buyer receives a late quotation. The quotation is for identical quality, identical service and delivery. The price? Instead of 20¢, it's 10¢. So what action would you take next time, if you were the buyer? Wouldn't you distrust your chosen supplier? Wouldn't you be determined to shop around next time to get the lowest price? Wouldn't you put extreme pressure on all suppliers to see if they are cheating you?

Most price wars are started by buyers. Sensing that the market is soft, and that the suppliers need the business badly, they search widely. Suppliers weaken on their prices in order to get the business. That makes the buyers even more determined. The news gets around and the war has started.

At first, buyers enjoy the price war; they enjoy their power. But later they come to hate it. It is time consuming, difficult and demanding. They are never sure they have the best deal. They long for a return to stability.

At first, the salesmen hate the price war. They suffer badly. Later, when they get power from their managements to deal on their own accord, they come to enjoy it. They enjoy the thrill, the hunt for new business at any price. They have an edge on their own management. "Do you want to do the business, or don't you?" they ask their chief. "Well then, you've got to give me the authority to deal at their price."

Here are eight rules for waging a price war through discounts, based on the principles enunciated by von Clausewitz in the 19th century for the waging of a real war.

1 Selection and maintenance of the aim

All military commanders must select and clearly define their aim. Each phase of a war will have a limited aim, and every plan of action must be tested by its bearing on the chosen aim. This is the Master Principle of Waging War.

All special deals, price cutting, extra discounts, bonus offers, rebates, promotional allowances, should be able to stand up to the rigid question: Why? One of the most remarkable statements to be made by company chairmen during the recession in the early 1980s was "We are cutting our prices to protect our cash flow." Would someone please explain how the cash flow is protected if the total money to be received is less than the total money to be paid out?

What is sometimes meant is that the company is sitting on very high stocks of finished product. The management calculates, then, that it will pay them to clear out the stock at lower prices and thereby increase their cash.

Now that is a specific aim, very laudable, and the action can be tested against it. British Leyland led a price fight through discounting in May 1980 in order to clear their new car inventory.

To keep a car in inventory for one month longer than necessary would cost them about 1½% of its inventory value in interest charges. So a car at an inventory value of, say, $8,000 is worth knocking out a little cheaper if it sells faster than it otherwise would. To have it standing in the showroom costs someone $120 a month.

Providing a car sells one month faster, the seller can afford to give away up to $120. More than that, and he has lost money.

But the deals offered to buyers of new cars in the spring of 1980 were up to 10% off the retail price!

With heavy inventories and a shortage of demand, a price fight in the car industry was inevitable. Actually, BL knew what it was doing. It knew that the first one to launch the inevitable attack would gain more ground. So it started the war everyone knew was coming.

That year BL's losses were horrendous—and so were the losses of the rest of the industry. Some companies hardly recovered their previous ground, but Ford, the market leader, tended to discount less, kept quieter about its offers, and by the end of 1981, had put on more market share than any other major company.

To gain new customers would be a laudable aim for heavy discounting. To secure demonstrations and sampling of the product by new users, would be laudable and specific aims for discounting.

To "force" distributors to stock the product would be a reasonable aim, although possibly storing up a problem for the future.

What actually happened in the British car industry during the price fight of 1980 and 1981 was predictable. With a shortage of money in consumers' pockets and rising unemployment in the United Kingdom, many ordinary people deferred their purchases of new cars. Fleet car buyers in industry also made their existing cars last longer to ease the financial strain on their capital budgets.

The special offers of spring 1980 simply pulled forward some latent demand. They robbed the future. There was a marked effect on new car sales in the

---

Figure 8.1
The principles of waging war

1　Select and maintain the aim.
2　Use surprise.
3　Maintain morale.
4　Take offensive action.
5　Secure your defenses.
6　Maintain flexibility.
7　Use a concentration of force.
8　Use minimum of effort.

Figure 8.2
The do's and don'ts of discounting

DO	DON'T
Keep your aim in mind.	Offer discounts because everyone else does.
Make surcharges if they won't pay.	Offer settlement discounts if there is another way of getting yourself paid.
Be creative with your discounting.	Copy everyone else.
Use discounts to clear stocks.	Discount when there is no need.
Put time limits on the deal.	Publish discounts for all time.
Discount for extra business.	Let them stick in the dealer's pocket.
Make sure discounts are passed on.	Give them away automatically.
Discount only to survive in a mature market.	Discount with a new product.
Use different discounts for different groups.	Use one discount for all purposes.
Keep flexibility, keep reviewing.	Let the boss give the money away.

spring, and then the market died. By the year end, the market was stagnant. Area sales managers for the car companies were then desperately forcing their dealers and distributors to stock; the dealers were equally desperate not to stock. In January 1981 morale was very low in the trade. But the demand was beginning to flow through the chain again. By August 1981, dealers were reporting record sales of new cars.

If you are going to discount heavily, or start a price fight, then whatever you do, carefully work out the effects of your action over the long term. That way, when you make the move, you will do so under controlled conditions.

Be concerned about von Clausewitz's major principle of war. Select and then maintain your aim.

Von Clausewitz did not rank any of his other principles in any order of merit—in applying them to the price war, we will not either.

2 Surprise

In war, surprise is a most effective and powerful weapon. By the use of surprise, results out of all proportion to the effort can be obtained. The elements of surprise include originality, audacity and rapidity, said von Clausewitz.

Be creative and original about your offers. How dull to offer just 10% off your list price. How very dull and very predictable.

Catch competitors with the unexpected. A management course was offered to businessmen with a standard discount of 20%, if five places were booked. Later, the same course was offered with a free place for one person, if four places were booked. The second offer tripled the number of multiple bookings. It's much more exciting to offer a *free* place. Get them excited.

Many people would like to run a railway. But few would be as ingenious or as creative as British Rail (yes, it's not a misprint, British Rail), when it comes to making special offers or discounts. Railways have a high fixed cost. Once the timetable is set up, it costs them virtually no more to carry a passenger once for 100 miles than it does to carry the passenger four times for 400 miles. What they want is to force passengers to use the railway more, and to use it automatically. In addition, they want to stop the passenger from always asking "shall I go by car or by train?" by selling him an annual season ticket. They give big discounts on annual season tickets anyway, but in exchange they get their cash up front. Many people buy quarterly tickets to spread the cost. But if you buy an annual season ticket on British Rail, you can travel anywhere in Britain or on weekends at half fare, and take up to four children at a flat rate of $1 each. Other fare concessions are also offered. None of them cost British Rail very much; without a doubt, many more people do buy annual season tickets. A little business is switched from the full-fare passenger who would travel on weekends anyway, but very little. That kind of discount is creative and ingenious. Much better than the tired old "10% off."

We can describe four basic types of discount. A *cash discount* might be offered for payments made on time. To be effective, the discount usually has to be on the order of 2½%. But if that pulls the money in one month faster than it would otherwise, then you are paying your customers an interest rate of 30% per annum. That rate is so high it would pay you if they did not take the discount and took one month longer to pay! It is often the most expensive money you use. No wonder some customers take all the settlement discounts offered, and even then some of them do not make the payments on time.

> Awkward question: *Why should you have to pay customers extra to complete their side of the bargain, when you have already done yours? Is it just because you are afraid of them?*

How much better to change your business terms so you can penalize them if they are overdue. How much better to eliminate the settlement discount and use a trained operator on the telephone to collect your overdue money. Suppose you are paying 20% for the most expensive money you borrow. If each telephone call costs you $2, and you are successful one time out of two in collecting your money one month faster, then you can afford this method on all accounts owing you more than $250. Above this figure, you have extra profit in the bank. The bad way is to offer a settlement discount; your costs go up in line with the size of customers' to you. By using an established telephone routine, you have a reasonably fixed cost per call. Hit the big accounts with the telephone. Avoid a cash or settlement discount if you can; use it only if you can prove beyond all doubt that it works better than anything else. (And even then, don't believe you cannot find a cheaper way.)

Quantity discounts are most common in industry. Some companies publish their quantity discounts. That way they give them away to everyone. Other companies do not give quantity discounts at all. One knitwear maker does not offer discounts to shops that buy in bulk. What they want is a range of high quality outlets. What they do not want are outlets that will offer price cuts on their expensive cashmere sweaters. That disturbs their market. Therefore big

---

Figure 8.3
Why offer quantity discounts?

To pass on the reduced costs of selling, packing, delivery or manufacturing that larger orders make possible.

To facilitate sale of weak products by applying discount to entire line.

To reward customers for continued business or exclusive dealing.

To reduce stock of slow-moving items.

To spur lagging sales.

To encourage concentration of purchases.

QUANTITY DISCOUNTS HAVE THREE MAJOR DRAWBACKS

1. Toward the end of a specified discount period, buyers may place larger orders to qualify for discounts. That may disrupt the production process and rob future sales.

2. There will be many requests for discounts from customers buying just short of the "break" point. For example, if the quantity over which a discount is given is 1,000 and a company buys 975, they may demand the discount.

2. They tend to remain in effect and are difficult to alter.

customers and small are charged the same amount. And the company makes the policy stick.

Other suppliers do not publish quantity discounts, but they will negotiate them. That is the best policy because it leaves your options open. Leave yourself room. Give yourself the chance to say, "If you do something for me, then I can give you an extra discount." By publishing your discounts you give away this lever. Actually, even if you publish your discounts, your very big customers will want an extra discount on top. So if the traditions of your industry are such that you must publish quantity discounts, then publish relatively small discounts (leaving yourself room for bargaining), and also vary your "breaks" on order size from those of your competitors. In this way, customers will find it difficult to compare your discounts directly with the competitors' discounts.

> Awkward question: *Why give customers a discount for giving you their normal order? No, save your discount for when they do something really special, such as making you sole supplier.*

Promotional discounts

Here is a rich variety of opportunities for waging limited war on the competitors. There is one basic rule to follow, however. Put a specific time limit on all discounts you offer for promotional purposes. Otherwise your promotion discounts will become embedded in your price-list structure, and you will have difficulty later when you try to stop the discount or alter it.

Make sure promotional discounts do the job you want them to do. If they are to motivate a customer to sell more for you, then make sure he *sells* more of your product. Otherwise he will take the bigger order into his inventory, do nothing with it, then reduce his order from you in the following month. You will have gained nothing at all.

He will have gained your promotional discount without having done anything at all to earn it. Don't use a promotional discount to sell *in*; use it to sell *through*. You should be able to prove that discounts for promotional purposes are working.

It is easy for things to go wrong with discounting; like having an unhappy love affair, it is easier to talk your way into it, than it is to talk your way out. That leads to another great principle of war.

3 The maintenance of morale

Everyone prefers stability and reasonable firmness. Buyers respect it in salesmen. Salesmen respect it in their management. Nothing is worse than a discount policy based on fear. Little will undermine a salesman's confidence more than a management decision based solely on matching the competition. If you want to destroy a salesman, and yourself, all you have to do is tell him that he must find out what the competition is bidding at, and then tell the buyer that whatever the price is, he will beat it.

Here is a further factor to maintaining morale. When the salesman calls in his boss to close the deal, the boss must never give the buyer a discount that is more than the salesman offered. Yet most sales bosses do just exactly that; and by doing so they cut the arms and legs from the field salesmen. From that moment on, the buyer wants to deal with the sales boss only—he knows he can get better results that way. Some sales managers like to show off their authority and status by being able to grant bigger discounts. That is a disastrous practice.

One area sales manager for a franchise negotiates new sites and renewals every five years with his franchise holders. When a franchise holder for an area gets very tough over the demands for capital investment and such, he may insist on seeing the sales director instead of just the area sales manager. The area sales manager warns the franchise holder that his director is a very difficult man, but if he wants to see him, he will arrange it.

When the sales director attends the meeting he is polite and charming. But, apparently, there is something about the deal that he does not like. He expresses doubt about a particular concession the area sales manager has already made. Far from giving in to the customer's extra demands, the sales director indicates that the company cannot hold to the area manager's promise: He is sorry but he will have to rethink the deal completely.

The customer is now perturbed at losing the deal altogether. The area manager restores the concession later and closes the deal. The customer never wants to meet the sales director again and would always prefer to deal with his area manager. The point is that all extra offers, all extra deals should go through the man handling the business—they should never come directly from the chief. And from time to time the company must stand firm on its price. That will give the salesman confidence in his own management team. It takes courage to fight a price war. And you are bound to lose the odd skirmish here and there.

4 Offensive action

So far, we have spoken mostly of defense—but there is a time in war to take offensive action. Until the initiative is seized, the aim cannot be accomplished. That does not mean "attack at any price." It means that there is a moment for the attacker to gain the advantage, and exploit it.

In nuclear defense theory, the idea is that the major powers would have a warning of an impending attack through behavioral signals of one kind or another. Threats, warlike verbal attacks, the manufacture of an international crisis, aggressive postures—those are the signals of impending war. It would be very difficult for a nation suddenly to launch a nuclear war without any warning at all. The attack on Pearl Harbor was a surprise, but it was undertaken in unstable world conditions with a major war being fought in Europe. Most nuclear strategies are based on a minimum of ten days "notice" being given. (That should relieve us all considerably!)

And so it is with a price war. Depressed demand will often combine with high inventories, and a production-line flow that cannot be stopped. Often short of money themselves, big customers hold back on their orders. Cash-flow problems, extra borrowing from the banks and spare industry capacity—the combination of all these factors will cause the pressure to erupt. Something has to give. And the something that gives is price. The war has started.

The life-cycle theory shown in Figure 6.4 is a very useful indicator of when, in a market, a price fight will break out.

After the initial phase of launching and market growth, the market takes a downturn, and the industry has idle capacity. If the idle capacity is of the kind that can be turned easily to other things, a price fight is less likely. But if capacity is inflexible, if the fixed costs are high, so the penalty for shortage of sales volume is severe, then price fights break out.

First, the quality of the backup service is damaged, as companies try to save money. A large number of different product varieties enters the market as companies search for pockets of demand not completely satisfied by the existing products. There is a fight for distribution as big buyers play off one company against another. Prices are low, profits are low, discounts and special offers are high.

Once the product life cycle is recognized, some action can be planned in advance for the inevitable pressure points. A new generation of improved products can be held in readiness to fight off competition. The company can take the lead in selected areas of the market to fight its price battles. The company can plan when to hold off and when to attack. And the company can also learn that most valuable lesson of all—when to get out altogether.

5 Security
Early in 1981, ICI found itself in considerable market difficulty in its manufacture of acrylic plastic sheets. Plastic producers in the United Kingdom charge much more to their fabricator customers than do the importers. The ICI product is up to 20% more expensive than European products, and the company claims that fluctuating exchange rates are the cause of the problem. ICI was reported to have planned to cut its price of extruded sheets by 10% to distributors. But distributors complained that such a price reduction would do no good, because competition would still be cheaper and ICI would gain no more business. The distributors were worried that the price cut might be carried over to another part of the market where ICI has a strong hold still, and has no need to cut prices. That was the market for cast sheets—the Perspex market.

As von Clausewitz might put it, a sufficient degree of security against enemy attack is essential in order to pursue the offensive aim. That means the defense of vital targets. Security does not imply undue caution or the avoidance of all risks: sometimes bold action is necessary.

In the ICI case, the distributors were undoubtedly right. In one sector of the market, ICI has a very strong hold and there is little price cutting. But in the extruded sector of the market, competion is very active indeed. Fighting competition with relatively small price cuts of 10%, the distributors felt, would not achieve their aim in this market, and might spread discounting into the more profitable market.

One-fifth of your products produce four-fifths of your gross profit. One-fifth of your markets or applications produce four-fifths of the business. One-fifth of your customers produce four-fifths of your company sales. Whether it is 20% producing 80% of the results, or 15% producing 90% does not matter; the principle remains the same: You can afford to ignore virtually four-fifths of your products and four-fifths of your customers and your market applications, because they hardly matter to your business.

But you must concentrate your attention where the bulk of your business is done. Thus there's a strong case for selective prices: flexible pricing to suit different applications in the market. Different prices may be needed to suit different territories. Different prices are needed to suit different product groups. Why give a discount over all your business? Why not vary your discounts from product group to product group? Different prices must be selected for different customers, particularly for your key accounts. Promotional discounts can then be placed where they will have most effect—right up against the immediate potential in each account. That adds up to a policy of security. Your flanks are defended, and your discounts are put to work where they will do the most good.

Look after your key customers—that's a good principle. While the OPEC nations were desperately trying to hold up the world price of oil to $41 a barrel during the recession, they faced the fact that the Rotterdam spot market, Saudi Arabia and Britain, were selling at lower prices. So Egypt cut the price of oil for Israel twice within a month to bring it to the spot-market price. Israel is Egypt's largest customer for oil. Peru offered a price reduction to Japan for its oil. Japan asked for $31 a barrel, Peru argued strongly and they settled at $33.25 a barrel. That, despite the fact that a contract existed to supply oil at an even higher price annd Peru could hold Japan to it. The reality was that Japan takes up practically all of Peru's surplus exports of oil. Peru was looking after its best customer.

6 Flexibility

This illustrates another of von Clausewitz's great principles of war: flexibility. Prearranged plans may have to be altered to meet changing situations. In marketing, as in war, the unexpected often happens. To be flexible, the company needs good training, organization, discipline and staff work.

From time to time you will need rapid decisions. At a time of a price war in the market, the information flow back to the company must be fast, accurate and reliable. The information flow also needs to get to the top of the business easily, without being filtered at the middle-management level.

Not many companies have the capacity to compete with a rapidly changing situation, and to seize fleeting opportunities. The bureaucracy gets in the way. Don't let it.

7 Concentration of force

To achieve success in war, it is necessary to concentrate forces superior to those of the enemy when the time and place are decisive.

So it is with a price war. If your discounts are strong enough to destroy your competition in the market; if you can then afford to advertise them so widely that you overwhelm the opposition; if your market is demonstrably price sensitive so that competitors have no distinctive product advantage over you; and if you can afford to do all of this and still leave yourself with plenty of profit to keep your company running—even if your discounting does not succeed—then you may consider the ultimate. You may consider starting a price war, from which your competitors must never be able to recover. Otherwise don't start the war.

Suppose you are caught up in a war and need to fight smaller battles. How much force do you need to apply to the market to make it move in your direction?

Most people massively overestimate the power of a price offer or a discount to move the market. When the market buys narrowly differentiated products, then it will change its buying pattern for relatively small differences in price. This is particularly true where little brand loyalty exists. If what you offer is vastly different, then the power of discounts to move sales is very limited.

There is some evidence from consumer markets on that point. It indicates that price cuts of less than 10%, in the average consumer product market will move very little extra. As the discount moves higher, toward the 13% to 15% level, the market can be expected to move significantly, but the share of the market gains may not be maintained as competitors respond. The market will move even more if you offer 18%. But you cannot guarantee that the sales gain will be maintained if the deal comes off, or if competitors respond equally.

Other evidence shows that it is more effective to offer deals on fast-selling lines than on slow-selling lines. Retailers find it more effective to offer deals on brand leaders rather than on small brands (Blattbert et al, "Price Deals for Non-Durable Goods," *AMA Journal of Marketing*, Winter 1981). A study showed that both retailers and consumers will increase their stockholdings of products if they are offered on a deal, only to reduce their total purchases later.

To break a recent recession, most major stores offered very deep price cuts of up to 30%, using special tie-in deals with their suppliers. Woolworths' held a major conference for its suppliers and told them the company policy would be to use only suppliers who were prepared to give them very deep price cuts which they could pass on to the public. They called it their "Crackdown" campaign. As a result, their retail sales volume during the early part of the year held up very well, despite the recession. During the recession retailers found a larger sales volume during the time of their annual sales, and so those were kept running longer. But retail groups can do that because even during sales they take their normal margins; they just pass their price cuts back to their suppliers by demanding very deep discounts.

The British cross-channel ferry operators followed the same price-cutting tactics in 1980, and were forced to do so again in 1981. The operator who started the price war, European Ferries, was saying by June 1981, that fares across the channel were too low. The chairman said, "Unless something happens within eighteen months, a significant number of operators will go out of business. The position is very dangerous at the moment." And he was the man who started the war!

The total market for cross-channel passengers was hardly affected by the price war. All that happened was that operators threw money at each other and all reduced their profits. From Dover in June of 1981, ships sailed within a few minutes of each other less than 20% full. Later the market picked up a bit. The ferries had become more efficient and offered better service to stave off the threat of a tunnel across the Channel. So the price war had one good effect in the end, but the process took nearly three years.

While all this was going on, a different fight was taking place in London's High Street. For many years, the supermarket chain Tesco, and its competitors, have used a small number of products as loss leaders. Tesco forced the pace of supermarket development in the United Kingdom in the early years. It offered these selected lines at extremely low prices, making deals with manufacturers who were persuaded by the offer of substantial volume sales; Tesco cut its own profit margins wafer-thin. The market came to their stores in the millions. Tesco built a solid reputation for low-cost products that has lasted until today. Reports indicate that in recent years, the lowest prices overall have been offered most frequently by Waitrose and by J. Sainsburys. But Tesco still holds the low-price reputation in the public mind.

But the loss-leader policy upsets the rest of the High Street trade. From lawn mowers to paints, salesmen constantly have to explain away to other customers the very low prices of their products offered on promotion by Tesco. The promotions do affect the market—there is no doubt about that. In April, 1981, the paint brand Magicote was being used as a loss leader by Tesco. Bergers, the manufacturers, said that Tesco was damaging its name in the market, its products, and its hundreds of other distributors. Determined to safeguard its market position, Bergers stopped supplies to Tesco, after consulting lawyers.

It is the first time this has been done to Tesco. And it will not be the last. By concentrating the force of their discounts on selected items which are promoted hard, Tesco has earned its overall reputation for low prices.

8 Economy of effort

To wage war requires a certain balance for the employment of forces. A judicious expenditure of effort is required to meet the needs of concentration and of security. How then should the balance be maintained in a discounting plan?

Here is a procedure for discount and promotion planning. First, decide upon your total advertising and promotion budget. Then divide it broadly between the items that you *must* spend money on: literature, packaging, direct mail or whatever it is that keeps your business moving. Then balance the remainder between your theme advertising requirement and your promotional requirement. Perhaps 70% to advertising, if you are a brand leader building loyalty in a stable market. Or perhaps 80% to sales promotion, if you are fighting hard for distribution in a fragmented market with depressed demand. The more industrial or technical your product, the more you should provide promotional support as close to the selling effort as possible: shows, demonstrations, exhibitions and the like.

Now you have your promotional budget set. Divide it into selling and promotional periods, perhaps six periods a year to tie in with your sales trip cycles, if you have them. That gives you six chunks of promotional spending, the logic of which products you should be supporting at different times of the year is self-evident.

Now here comes the plan that will balance your effort. In any given period of two months, back one product heavily with a major promotion scheme. Support it with advertising, and work hard at spreading the news of the scheme or of heavy discounts to your customers. At the same time, provide your salesmen with two minor discount or promotional schemes. They involve less money, and achieve more limited objectives, but they give your salesmen help. It means that your salesmen always have something extra to push. Your promotional discounts will vary from time to time, and that is a good thing.

You can tailor-make your discount efforts to suit your specific market objectives; to defend your position in a market here; to try to get new products stocked there; to get new customers and new business in another promotion period.

Figure 8.4
Four steps in discount promotions planning

1   Decide your total advertising and promotion budget.

    Allocate your basic expenses, literature etc.

    Allocate your proportion to theme advertising.

    Allocate your proportion to promotional support.

2   Divide your promotional budget into sales trip cycles

    Tie in with product support.

    Tie in with advertising support.

    Tie in with sales aim.

3   In each period run one major and two minor promotions

    Plus discounts to new customers.

    Plus discounts to force existing volume.

    Plus settlement, quantity, standard discounts.

4   Negotiate special deals, each period, big customers

Figure 8.5
The Nuts and Bolts of Promotion Planning

SALES PERIOD ONE

Level
of
expense

Nuts	Bolts	Screws	Washers
Heavy advertising	Competition to buyers	Discounts for display	No promotion

SALES PERIOD TWO

Level
of
expense

Nuts	Bolts	Screws	Washers
No promotion	Free bolts offered as samples	Free screw with every washer bought	On-pack offer with screws

SALES PERIOD THREE

Level
of
expense

Nuts	Bolts	Screws	Washers
Special bonus margin to trade	No promotion	New product launch (with left-handed thread)	Buy two washers, get one free

A lighthearted look at promotion and discount planning to support the selling effort in a company making nuts, screws, bolts and washers.

The purpose is to demonstrate the means by which all these activities can be tied in to a central plan that covers a full range of marketing objectives with all products, yet at the same time allows for flexibility, surprise, and for an economy of effort.

One further thing. Try to relate your promotion discounts for particular customers to the *extra* volume business they can do for you over and above their normal business. Suppose you make a 30% gross profit margin on 10 tons of product to one customer who is triple sourcing—buying his supplies from three companies. If you can knock out one competitor completely, you might sell him, say 20 tons instead. You can give a promotional discount of up to 30% off the price of the extra 10 tons to get the business without losing any money, provided it does not push you into extra production costs, overtime, or delivery charges. A 30% discount on the extra volume is a very big discount (too big actually). You would have to limit it to the *extra* volume, and to be certain the customer did not want you to reduce your price on your existing volume. You would have to make sure the rest of the market does not hear of the deal. You would also have to maintain your integrity, and provide a sound reason why you can offer this extra 30% on this occasion. And you will have to have a plan to get the customer back to normal discounts on the total business as quickly as you can. But provided all these criteria can be met (most of them probably cannot), then you could offer big discounts on the extra volume only. Most companies do not use the principle of giving big discounts and limiting them to the *extra* business above the normal. But if it is genuine extra business for you, then it is a very judicious use of your money. Provided it does not start a price war, of course.

> Proverb for discounters: *He who is strong enough to start a price war may not be strong enough to stop it.*

HOW TO MINIMIZE THE DAMAGE CAUSED BY A PRICE WAR

1 Make sure the demand is stronger than the supply
During a recession you must move. It is fatal to stand still. You are going to move in the end anyway because the market will shift you if you don't move voluntarily.

You can move either upmarket or downmarket. You can add either extra value or strip the product to its core and sell it cheap. As a recent recession began, the price of professional chain saws nearly halved in one year, despite the fact that inflation was running at 15%. The market expanded quickly, despite the recession in other garden-equipment markets. Equally, when a recession is over, a company can either retrench its facilities and cut itself back to a tight central cost, or it can expand massively in order to gain market share. One company spent substantial capital in developing a new range of earth-moving equipment during a recent recession. Having protected its cash and profits, it went for a tremendous increase in market share when the recession ended.

Whatever you do, whether you move up or you move down, remember the golden rule that you should try to be certain that the demand in the market will, in the long run, exceed your resources. That way it puts you in a position of power and control. Your order books will be full and you will get the prices you want with minimum discount.

If your cash flow is good, and your profit record is excellent so you can borrow money in the market should the need arise, and provided the underlying trend in your market is towards growth, then it can pay you to expand your facilities, knock the price down radically and hammer the competition to the edge of the market. But to do so, you need a discount of at least 25% on the normal selling price in the marketplace, and you may need much more than that. It requires strong nerves and great courage, but the profits can be considerable.

The alternative is to cut the business back, concentrating on the things you do extremely well and getting rid of all the marginal activities, positioning yourself in a specialized position in the market.

2 Work your margins and your price
In desperation, to minimize the losses caused by a severe price fight, carry out the following actions:

1 Strip away every item of spare cost on the central product under attack. You must get the bare product price down in order to compete with, and hold, competitive volume; strip all the associated services and back up from it.
2 Charge extra for everything connected with the product: delivery, installation, service, consulting, commissioning. Make extra charges for special favors, and strip the credit facility away. Offer the economy package, the bare bones of the product with everything else charged as an extra; or the deluxe package, with all the services plus a few extras. That way your customers will have a choice, and your salesmen have something with which to compete.
3 Walk around your stock room, your warehouses. Examine the product range in detail. Raise the small products in price. Raise the slow-moving products in price. Raise the add-on products in price. Raise everything you can but keep the central price-fight product down in price—let the rest of the range pay for it.
4 Look at your invoices. List out all the things you could possibly charge into them. Could you charge for telephone calls, administration, handling, telexes, storing? Have this list of items printed on your invoices and then pick up the costs separately and charge them out.
   You might easily find an extra 5% or more from this alone.

Notice that we are talking about the problem of your company's survival. We do not normally need to be so aggressive, but in a price fight the pressure is severe, and the margins are so thin that they must be worked hard.

It is not a technique designed to build respect and authority. It is damaging to a company's reputation, but in an extreme situation companies at the margin of survival will adopt the practice of, "Buy it and cook it." The procedure is to price as low as is necessary to land the business, then having landed it, work up all the extras afterwards. Add extra services, sell more volume to the account, tie them up. Builders know the technique well. Ask a roofing specialist for a quotation for a new garage roof, and the average small jobber will give you a low price. As soon as he has gotten the old roof off, he will show you how the joists have sunk, how the wood has rotted and how the rain cannot drain effectively because the central joist is not strong enough for the job. "Whoever built your garage did a hurried job on it. Took shortcuts. What do you want us to do?" What will you do? You'll pay up, that's what you'll do.

And very large building contractors will use the same technique, if they have to, when bidding for contracts against low price competition.

HOW TO STOP A PRICE WAR

Unless you have a 60% share of the market or more, you are unlikely to stop it. And even then you might not be able to do so. Your only alternative, if you have a lower market share, is to persuade two or three companies whose shares adds up to 70% or more of the market, that it is in everyone's interest to stop it. That may run afoul of antitrust law, but if the alternative is going broke, then some companies will do it.

Two styles are available to you. Both involve high risk. You can do what a timber company did. You can threaten to cut your prices by twice as much as your competitors. The timber company carried out this threat, which no one believed, and took the fight directly to his competitor's major customers. It took him two years to stop the price war and he nearly went to the wall financially, but he did it and the market stabilized.

You can do it through collaboration, as the U.S. steel companies did under President Nixon. The government wanted the steel companies to compete during a recession by cutting prices. The steel companies refused, because they had long memories going back to the 1930s when they did exactly that and they all nearly went out of business. The U.S. steel industry has had a hard time during the 1970s as a result of the non-price-cutting policy, but they have survived and made some money without calling on their government to bail them out—yet. That contrasts with the European steel companies that threw money at each other in 1974/5 and again in 1980/81. The break-even point for steel production is 80%. If you are selling more than four-fifths of your production capacity then you make money. Less than that, you lose horribly. The steel companies were selling only 50% of their capacity. Then they cut prices against each other. No one bought more steel. All that happened was that the European governments had to bail out their biggest companies with enormous subsidies. Otherwise their countries would have had no steelmaking capability at all. That's unthinkable.

One marketing professor, D. S. Leighton (*New Developments in Pricing Strategy*, 1967), has noted that group behavioral responses are necessary to resolve unstable market situations. Resolving price wars requires a significant and respected leader of the market to indicate the way, and a mature set of relationships in which each competitor acknowledges and respects the qualities of the others in particular sectors of the market. Prices are stabilized as a result of competitors having a shared interest in the future of the market as a whole. There must also be a willingness among everyone to penalize deviant behavior on the part of one member.

Price wars exhaust themselves in the end. Mergers push dying companies together. Capacity is reduced. Companies begin to behave sensibly, others pull out of the industry. And when the price war is over, everyone heaves a sigh of relief.

ITT and Union Carbide must decide what to do about the international capacitors market. If they follow the collaborative course, they cannot be sure that the importing companies from the Far East will join them and stabilize prices. If they threaten to attack the market with prices below the costs of production, they cannot be sure the importers won't simply withdraw from the market for a time, and then come back in again when prices rise later. Put simply, they are stuck with a very nasty dumping situation which will probably trundle on for many years to come.

In the next few years, perhaps, there will probably be less frenzy in the market for capacitors.There will be reduced tension, and everyone will cope with aggressive pricing by quietly exhausting themselves. It will peter out in the end. Some wars are like that.

SUMMARY

Caught in a price war you must decide whether you can influence the total behavior of the market, or get out altogether, or minimize the damage the price war can do to you.

You must have strong market power to be able to influence the competition, or be able to put the power together through an industry association. Then you threaten, cajole, lead and, where necessary, punish the others to conform.

If you are going to get out altogether, then the quicker you do so the better. While you are getting out you can strip costs to the bone in order to rescue whatever profits can be rescued.

If you are going to make the best of it, then do so in three ways. First, trim your organization down very tight, as quickly as you can. It is very uncomfortable, and you will dislike it, but every minute you save will add to your survival chances. Then get your administration, service, and routine working really efficiently. Set up high standards of performance—that will give you an edge in the market, because everyone else's performance will be falling off. Finally, work your margins in every way possible. Examine your invoices. Break up what you offer into small packages so you can compete with low prices if you have to. Use two-tier pricing: a standard low-cost package, and a deluxe version with all the additional services. Cross your fingers, and good luck. You may emerge as the richest operator in the industry.

Making Price Changes to Force Your Market Share and Profits | 9

Before reading the chapter, complete the answers to these questions in the spaces on the left-hand side. Then without looking at the answers, read the chapter. Finally, complete the answers again, making any changes you think fit. Score both sets of your answers. This tells you how much the chapter has affected your opinion. Scores are at the end of the book (p. 199).

HOW DO YOU RATE AS A BUSINESSMAN?

Q.1 *You are a regional brewer. The sales of your brewery's beer are 4% below last year's and your net profits are down from 16% on sales to a mere 13%. The barley harest was poor and your material costs are expected to go up by 14% in the next few months. Materials account for 55% of your total costs. All your competitors are facing the same squeeze on prices, costs and sales. At the meeting of the local brewers committee you are expected to advise your competitors about proposed price increases. What will your advice be? General inflation is running at 11% in the economy.*

(a) Everyone should raise their prices by 12% at one time, as soon as possible; (b) all wait for a bit to see how the market goes; (c) all plan for two increases of about 7% each, one now and another in four months' time; a third increase afterward if necessary; (d) encourage each of the others to make his own decision about raising prices, while secretly you plan to lower yours.

Score   **Score**

                        Before reading chapter.   *After reading chapter.*

Q.2 *Your meat pies are mouth-watering when they are fresh-baked in your big traveling oven. Three days later, and after refrigeration, it's another matter. However, you sell more meat pies than anyone else in the area. What would be your general attitude toward your competitors in this fairly price sensitive market?*

(a) Each competitor should have his own policy. You deal with competitors as you find them; (b) you tell them off gently when they sell pies at very low prices; (c) if they undercut you, you threaten them with demolition of their key accounts; (d) you attack the competition on price as hard as you can.

115

Score   **Score**

Before reading chapter.   *After reading chapter.*

———   ———

Q.3   The delivery and distribution cost of your soft drinks forms 20% of your total
wholesale price. You have just made a deal with the drivers for a 16% raise
to prevent them from joining the union, and your gasoline costs have gone
up by 10% in the past three months. Your net profits are wafer-thin at 2%
on turnover. You need a 3% price increase quickly to break even with no
loss of sales.

(a) Your financial director wants to take the price increase across the board,
all products the same. You must maintain a consistent margin, he says; (b)
your marketing manager wants to increase prices product by product; some
increasing more, some less; (c) your sales director wants the price increase
only for the smaller customers, but says to leave the large customers' prices as
they are. Tell them the price increases are negotiable, he says; (d) your
production director wants a new bottling plant to reduce the labor cost.

*If you were running a contest for management judgment, out of five points,
how many would you give each of them? Five is top score.*

Score   **Score**

———   ———

Before reading chapter.   *After reading chapter.*

———   ———

Q.4   All your competitors are going up in price shortly. But they use sugar and
you use a high-fructose corn syrup that is about 5¢ per pound cheaper. Your
material costs are down while theirs are rising. They'll be going for a 7%
price increase or thereabouts. You could actually afford to reduce your prices
by 5% and still maintain your profit margins, but that would wipe out any
advertising allowance you built into your costs. What will you do? You have
15% share of a fragmented market.

(a) Raise prices along with the competition; (b) hold your prices level for a
while and go up later, perhaps; (c) pare your prices to the bone to win the
competition's business; (d) lower your prices for key accounts and new customers
by 2½%, and spend the rest on advertising your low prices.

Score   **Score**

———   ———

Before reading chapter.   *After reading chapter.*

———   ———

Q.5   One of the following statements is good policy; the other three represent poor
policy. Which is the good one?

(a) Never tell the customers your prices are going to go up, until the last possible minute; (b) never try to come to an understanding on price with your competitors, because it will not do any good, and they'll attack you with their lower prices; (c) always tell the customers that your proposed price increase would have been a lot bigger had it not been for the improvements you made to your business efficiency, and provide them with evidence of this; (d) don't try and buy your way around your key accounts with favorable terms on price increases.

Score   **Score**

_____   _____

Before reading chapter.   *After reading chapter.*

_____   _____

Q.6   *Your company is fully stretched financially, with a new project that will pay off in three years and that has taken you five years to develop. Your market is competitive and tight but expected to turn up in a year or so. You are overdrawn in excess of your limit with the bank. The manager has called you to pay the excess immediately; he wants to reduce your overdraft limit and take a debenture on your business. You have guaranteed the loan personally. Rank the top three of the following actions:*

(a) Selling off the development project immediately to raise funds; (b) cutting costs of all kinds; staff, overhead, everything you can think of; (c) raising the extra money from your aunt; (d) transferring all your personal assets to your wife's name, to reduce the bank's hold over you; (e) taking a second mortgage on your house, taking a loan against your insurance; (f) searching for a new project to make money quickly; (g) selling your premises and leasing them back to raise the money; (h) tightening your cash flows hard, taking longer to pay creditors, dunning customers to pay faster; (i) cutting your sales force, advertising, promotion costs; (j) raising your selling prices by as much as is needed to provide you with profits.

Score   **Score**

_____   _____

Before reading chapter.   *After reading chapter.*

_____   _____

Scores

26 +	Very good.
18–25	Fair.
12–17	Score it again in case you've missed something.
11 or less	Put it down to bad luck.

Making Price Changes to Force Your Market Share and Profits | 9

The year is 1770. You are the chief of a village in Bengal surrounded by paddy fields. There is a rice famine throughout the land, but in your village you have rice stocks built up. The crowd surrounding your house is in the thousands. Many have walked with their families and children for miles, since you are the only one with rice and they are desperate.

The government inspector is in the village to make sure you do not profit from the famine. If you sell your rice stocks above the government regulated price, then you will be prosecuted and, if proven guilty, you will be stoned and executed. So you sell all your stocks at the government regulated price. Your stocks are exhuasted within a few hours. Fights break out in the crowd. Rice is stolen from those lucky enough to have been in line early. In 1770, one-third of the population in Bengal died as a result of the rice crop failure being handled in this manner.

Ninety-six years later, the province of Bengal was again on the verge of a rice famine. But men in the government of the day were the great grandsons of those who issued the disastrous price-fixing policy in the previous famine. They were determined to avoid the earlier catastrophe. They reversed the policy completely; so completely that they actually encouraged and stimulated the rice farmers to get as much as they could for their crops. As a historian of the day reported, in 1866 respectable men in vast numbers went into the rice trade. The government assisted them by publishing weekly returns of the prices in each district, making the traffic both easy and safe. Everyone knew where to buy rice cheapest (where it was most plentiful) and where to sell it dearest. Food was brought from those districts that could most spare it, to those districts where it was most urgently needed. The distribution costs were paid for out of the higher prices. Certainly there was great hardship among the people, and some died from starvation. But the free market kept the disaster under control. The freedom to set prices effectively rationed supplies.

In the long run, a government policy that seeks initially to limit prices, must later extend into a system of rationing and distribution of supplies. It is inevitable then that the market must be told what it can consume. Because people have their own ideas of what they want, and some can afford to pay, they are reluctant to follow such directives except in times of crisis (such as wartime). So the directives must be backed by legislation with penalties for those who fail to conform. The impact on personal freedom can be judged any day in a Moscow shopping center with its long lines and inadequate products. The people who are not in lines are those in privileged positions—say in government—because in such economies secondary markets with plentiful supplies are established. Some of these markets are officially tolerated and are designed for the privileged. Others are called black markets, the penalties for trading in which are usually frightening for both buyer and seller.

Our system in the West is better. Here market forces prevail and we can adjust prices up or down relatively free of the law, constrained only by competition, demand and supply.

FIVE WAYS TO IDENTIFY A BUSINESS WRECKER

1 Business wreckers imagine market rumors to be true. They imagine competitors are undercutting them and always believe the customer who says their prices are too high.
2 Business wreckers believe that if their sales go down, then it must be due to the high price. They do not pay attention to their own market share; they do not analyze the total market figures.
3 Business wreckers always concentrate upon some prices to the exclusion of others; business wreckers never see that it is the total cash coming in minus the total cash going out that allows the business to run. A business wrecker thinks price changes should be due to cost changes only.
4 Business wreckers usually wait for crises to resolve themselves. They hold on to their positions at all costs, hoping for an act of God to turn their business around. The basis of their belief is that they offer the right price for all time.
5 Business wreckers are often honorable people who hold some notion of the right "moral" price and the right "moral" profit. Awful losses are put down to bad luck, and cannot be set off against huge profits which they believe to be unethical and so unearned.

INCREASING THE PRICE—LEADER OR FOLLOWER?

The ability to raise a price is to a large extent determined by the ability to control the supply into a given market.

If you want to buy platinum seriously, then sooner or later you must deal with Rio Tinto Zinc. The price will be determined by how much of the stuff they wish to dig out of the ground each year. They mine just as much as will keep the world platinum markets stable. They have no need to dig for more because that will only push up their profits, which will then be whisked away by various governments (of the countries in which they choose to take their profits) and, furthermore, it will drive down the world price of platinum. Control over the platinum price is easy for Rio Tinto Zinc.

If you produce bananas, you are in a more difficult situation than Rio Tinto Zinc. You will need to call a banana conference among all the producers and agree on a minimum selling price. That will not be easy because some banana producers are desperate for money; in other countries, the politicians may be coming up for reelection and they will not want to drive their economies down during the campaigns. After the election—well, that's a different matter. So a price-fixing agreement will be hard to make stick.

Even if you do get your banana floor prices fixed by agreement, the market will destroy you. Bananas suffer from two problems. First, they are not essential to anyone (except to the producers); people do not deeply care if their banana flambé is off the menu for a while. The second problem is more serious. Bananas are perishable. The customers will break a price cartel by leaving them to rot on the dock. They did exactly that in 1975, when the suppliers' cartel was formed. By 1976, the cartel was finished.

Nevertheless, it is along the track of competitive power that a company must look if it is to increase its prices.

Nearly half of the world's tin is produced in Malaysia. Over half of the world's tin is consumed in the United States and in Japan. For the prepackaging of some foods, there are few acceptable alternatives to tin. There is always some form of plastic, but the ecologists hate it, and its price rises with the price of oil. So tin it is, and Malaysia has the upper hand.

A series of international Tin Agreements are worked out each year to determine the floor and ceiling prices of the commodity. A consortium of consuming countries has been formed with the EEC prominent. Each year there are disputes among both the producers and the consuming countries.

With tin being a finite resource and growing more scarce, and with the strong demand and no adequate substitute, the price of tin will probably continue to rise in advance of other commodities year by year. At the end of the day there is only one price leader who determines the issue. That is Malaysia.

You become the price leader by being strong in the marketplace. The price leader is usually, but not always, the market leader. The price leader is the major producer whom the others respect for his knowledge and experience, and for the way he manipulates the market; or else they fear him and his retaliatory powers should they step out of line on price.

It is popular among left-wing economists to presume that markets are manipulated directly by the large multinational suppliers' rigging.

Overt market rigging happens much less often than the left wingers suppose. Monopolies commissions exist to fight such practices, but they are not overworked.

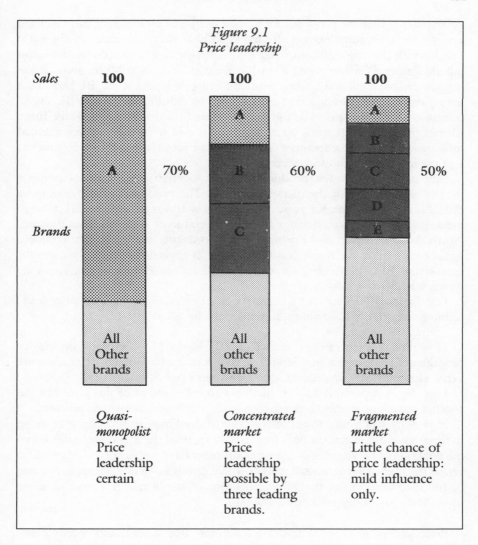

Figure 9.1
Price leadership

Sales   **100**   **100**   **100**

                             A   A
                                                  B
         A   70%   B   60%   C   50%
                                                  D
Brands   C   E

         All   All   All
         Other   other   other
         brands   brands   brands

Quasi-   *Concentrated*   *Fragmented*
monopolist   *market*   *market*
Price   Price   Little chance of
leadership   leadership   price leadership:
certain   possible by   mild influence
                  three leading   only.
                  brands.

The fact is that the pressures for a price rise build up in an industry in such a way that most suppliers are affected equally at the same time. In the early 1980s, while the major oil companies were suffering nasty losses due to declining oil and gasoline consumption, a small price war broke out. Mobil accused the market leaders, Shell and Exxon, of price cutting. Within a week, BP had called for an end to the subsidies that are paid out to gasoline dealers by the major companies to enable prices at the pumps to be held down. At the same time, BP put pressure on its rivals by raising the price of industrial and commercial fuels by less than its competitors did. Esso had a lot to lose through this move; and the infighting was quite severe.

But, of course, if a few producers can get together quietly, they can often rig the market without the market knowing. The producers of paper pulp in the EEC countries have for years wondered how it was that their markets have been distorted by price offerings from pulp producers as far afield as Finland, North America, Spain and Portugal. Those countries rarely seem to compete against each other for major contracts; but it is alleged that they always unite against the EEC producers. Or so it seemed to the European Commission, which was looking into it.

For the individual company in the specialist market looking for a price leadership position, the following questions must be asked:

How much control can be exercised over the market? How far can competitors be influenced to move in line? How would such control or influence be exercised? What sanctions exist against someone who steps out of line?

How far is it possible for the customer to reject the price increase? Has he another source of supply to move to quickly? Is there a substitute product?

How long will it take to get into a price leadership position? Can it be done in three months? A giant supplier with 60% share of the market might achieve the goal simply by warning everyone of his moves and publicizing them widely. Or, in the case of a fragmented market where upward of a dozen suppliers must be prodded to conform, the influential approach might take five years or more to build the necessary respect for the leader.

Price leadership depends on having accurate information and speedy communications. The moment someone of significance makes a move on price or discount, the price leader must know instantly. He must feed back that knowledge to his competitors in the trade rapidly before they hear of it from other sources. That will increase his power. The competition may then become slightly dependent on him for such information.

In markets characterized by aggressive, hostile competitors, as many markets are, there is little hope of collaboration unless the three top competitors can share 60% of the specified market.

In all cases other than the establishment of price leadership, the individual supplier must make do with his own resources as best he can.

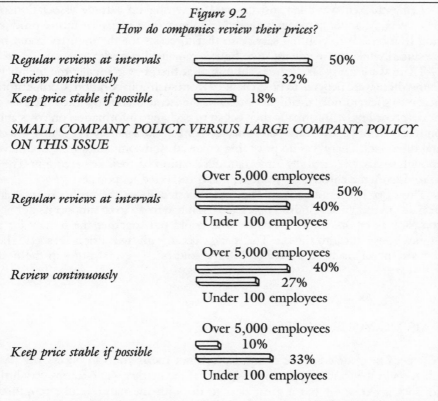

Figure 9.2
How do companies review their prices?

Regular reviews at intervals   50%
Review continuously   32%
Keep price stable if possible   18%

SMALL COMPANY POLICY VERSUS LARGE COMPANY POLICY ON THIS ISSUE

Regular reviews at intervals

Over 5,000 employees
50%
40%
Under 100 employees

Review continuously

Over 5,000 employees
40%
27%
Under 100 employees

Keep price stable if possible

Over 5,000 employees
10%
33%
Under 100 employees

Too many companies try to run their businesses on the basis of keeping prices stable. This is particularly true of small companies—it might even be one reason why they stay small. Prices need to be constantly examined; not changed all the time, but examined. Price is too important an issue to be left alone for long.

Suppose that shortly after the introduction of broiler chickens to grocery store shelves, Acme, one of the leading companies, within two years had 24% of the market. Initially, the product was launched at a slightly higher price than its competitors but advertising heavily.

Competitors serving the market attacked the new brand vigorously on price, but failed to stop its growing share of the market. The more they cut their prices against it, the more the customers remained loyal.

Acme chicken was then instrumental in setting up a trade association of producers. Member companies agreed to submit their plans for future production to a central accounting service so that forecasts for the industry could be produced while the members' own figures remained confidential.

There were many fake figures submitted at first, but gradually the members found there were benefits to be exchanged from such collaboration. Competitors began to shelter under the higher prices of the Acme brand and lifted their own prices accordingly. Informally they began to exchange information on costs and on methods of production. Later they exchanged information on selling prices and discounts. There was no price ring involved, and companies were not naive enough to disclose critically important information on their key accounts. They looked to Acme chicken for leadership and respected its policies.

The story has a sad ending. The trade boasted about the profits that could be made in the chicken industry—Acme felt it had to do so to support its public-company flotation. Soon, everyone who could put together the money for a broiler house got into the act. The market became glutted. Prices crashed. The industry never really recovered and Acme sold out—several times in the next few years.

RAISING YOUR PRICES

Just because your costs are rising, it does not mean you can necessarily pass them on in the form of price increases. What the market will bear has very little to do with costs; it has a great deal to do with the nature and strength of demand.

The first question to ask is whether your customer must absorb your price increase out of his own profits, or whether he can himself pass them on. He will resist, and resist strongly, any price increase coming out of his own pocket. His greatest resistance will be against the price increases of products that form a high proportion of his manufacturing costs.

In the autumn of the 1981 recession, the construction industry was suffering from very weak demand. Companies accepted price increases in line with inflation from a host of suppliers. But when it came to the price of cement, the customers said "no" very firmly. There had already been a price increase of 12% in March. A proposal to raise cement prices by 4 to 6% in July was scrapped after trade resistance. Prices would then have to rise by between 9% and 12% in November, said the cement makers. Over our dead bodies, argued the customers and started to set off one supplier against another. The biggest supplier of cement had 60% of the home market. It wanted a smaller increase than its competitors' because it could see its major customers making plans to buy in large quantities of cheaper cement from overseas. The last thing it wanted was for an importer to establish a bulk terminal in the heart of its market. Its smaller competitors needed a higher price increase badly.

The cement makers had to take the risk and force their prices up, because demand in the first six months was down 18%, and costs were rising. The squeeze was inexorable. But the big supplier won the day.

Its construction company customers could not easily pass on the price increases; they had to absorb most of them out of profits which weren't there. So they dragged imports in cheaply if they could, without a second thought to their normal suppliers. Many of them were delighted to do this because they remained incensed at a 24% price increase levied by the cement makers in the previous year. As a result, they formed a buyer's ring that put on great pressure. The cement market is going to change in the next few years. The penalty for handling price changes badly can be very high indeed.

> Question: *Who pays the bill for the price increase, your customer or your customer's customer? He'll fight you tooth and nail if he pays, but will just give you a hard time if someone else does.*

About the same time as the cement squabble, farmers were having a much easier time getting their demands for an increase in the price of liquid milk. There was some resistance here and there, a few rumors of dissent and the occasional statement of protest. But the price increase went through all right. Why? Because it could be taken out of increased retail prices for milk in the long run. It is easy to get price increases passed on when the other man does not care. But when the price increase might destroy his business, it becomes a little harder.

When the market shows signs of turning up or is in a boom period, that's the time to take the price increase. ICI needed an increase in the price of nylon and polyester for two years throughout their market and could not get it. Their profits were low, their costs were rising, they fired many thousands of workers to keep the company going. But they did not raise their nylon and polyester prices. Why? Because overcapacity among world suppliers, particularly among U.S. competitors, meant that plants were closing. To keep those plants afloat, orders were taken at any price. Otherwise ICI would have lost its business.

But at the very moment when all the marginal competitors had closed their plants, and the market showed very slight signs of an upturn, ICI decided to raise prices between 10% and 15%. They needed considerably more than that to break even, but it would do for a modest start.

In a multiproduct company facing a recessed market, price increases must be taken where they can be. Standard costs have nothing to do with it—if the Peter product has to be robbed to pay for the Paul product, then so be it. When Shell plants operated at only 55% of capacity for the production of polypropylene sold to the chemical industry, the prices were lower than those of a year earlier—a desperate bid to keep the plants open at any cost. Shell is the price leader. At the first opportunity, they raised prices, and their competitors followed suit with relief. That opportunity occurred when the market showed the first sign of an increase in demand. But other products were still held down to loss-making prices.

A SIX POINT GUIDE TO MAKING PRICE INCREASES

1 Raise prices when everyone else does
Hide yourself in the forest. Suppliers often make a great mistake by holding back on a price increase for a few weeks while the rest of the industry goes up, thereby hoping to gain an advantage in extra business. But the rest of the competition successfully persuades the trade that all the prices are going up, so the trade is reluctant to switch suppliers in the short term; second, when the supplier does increase his prices, he does so all by himself in a cold spotlight of attention. Many of his customers will think he has raised prices twice, and competitors will not disabuse them of that notion. Thirdly, the rest of the trade will not trust the supplier again. He will be cold shouldered from the councils of war.

Don't hold back: If the others are raising their prices, then you should go with them. The only exception to this is where you plan a penetration price technique, so that when the others go *up* you put your prices *down*, advertise them widely and aggressively, and make up your losses with increased volume. But that is the strategy of the brave, or the foolish. If you are going to do it, you must do it so fiercely that you can be certain of driving some of the

---

Figure 9.3
Minimum and maximum increases likely to be applied

Percentage	Minimum Increase	Maximum Increase
1 –2½	26	1
3 –5	68	9
5½–7½	1	6
8 –10	5	32
11 –15	–	32
16 –20	–	12
Above 21	–	8

Source: *How British Industry Prices*, Industrial Market Research, 1975

competition out of the business altogether, because they cannot afford to compete with you. If you have the resources of Fort Knox, then try it.

2 Not too much at any one time

People have a mental yardstick they use when checking prices. Move outside that measure and you will be subjected to cries of immorality, profiteering and all around greediness unless you can prove yourself innocent.

The common measure of an acceptable price increase is the general rate of inflation. Buyers will mentally tolerate price increases that are below or at the general level of price increases in the country. At that level, the need to demonstrate the case remains and buyers will always complain about the price increase proposed. But the increase will generally go through, provided other prices are moving by about the same amount.

Difficulty is experienced when a particular company or an industry as a whole needs to push up its prices significantly higher than the general rate of inflation. An increase in the price of an important commodity; a weakening of the currency; or a rapid surge in fuel costs may have a sharper impact on some industries than on others. If the price of silver increases, it is hardly the lead story in the business pages. (The price of gold is a much sexier story for journalists.) But if you are a professional photographer, you will read the news about silver prices with gloom—sooner or later it will affect your costs dramatically.

So if the industry must move with significantly higher prices than inflation, it must make a very sound case for it. It must also use warnings and signals in order to get the market used to the idea of forthcoming increases. A *Financial Times* story splashed the news that Britain's paintmakers expected prices to increase "by 35%" in the forthcoming year. The trade was horrified; general inflation was around 11% at the time. When the trade price increases finally came through, they totalled about 24% and the market was much relieved. Actually, the market had been set up beautifully.

If an individual company must move by itself and it is well out of line with inflation, and also well out of line with the rest of its industry, then it needs extreme care in handling.

3 Not too often

Keeping your head low when price increases are about is a good idea, and relatively small, but frequent increases, is one way of doing this. Over a period of time, regular buyers will notice if price increase notifications from the same supplier seem to come flooding through the door at short, regular intervals. How often is too often? Well, raising the prices once a week is too often.

Generally, a quarterly phasing seems to be as frequent as is acceptable for a company moving slightly higher than its competition. It is always a trade-off between frequency and size of increase. Many industries have a tradition of once-a-year increases across the board. While that provides good cover for a supplier, the routine is too inflexible and does not leave enough room for individual movements against the stream. There is always a lag between the time when a company's cost increases are incurred and the company's ability to put up the prices. The drag must be paid for out of profits. The problem is badly compounded when a company finds it must wait for a price increase until the annual move of the industry.

Get the customers used to small but fairly frequent shifts in price. Remember also that prices need not always move up; see next point.

4 Move something down when you move something up
Companies panic when they move prices. Their need for the extra money is uppermost in their minds, and they become insensitive to their customer's position. That's silly, very silly.

> Tip for marketing managers: *Search for a little oil to lubricate those parts of the customers' minds undergoing friction.*

Find some economy for them if you possibly can. Point out that there are cheaper products in your range that they can buy. Point out that they can buy smaller sizes if they want to keep their cash payments level. Point out that you have just *lowered* the price of one or two small products in your range. Wherever you can effect economies in production, then you should show that you will pass on the savings to them. It all helps to create less friction, and prevent seizing up. What is seizing up? When the customer throws out your price increase, and your product also, and buys from a competitor in your place—that's seizing up. Prevent it.

5 Look after your key accounts
Remember that 80% of your profits are in the hands of relatively few customers. You must pay attention to such customers. Give them advance notice, give them a chance to stock up at the old price. Find a way to give them a little more time than the others. The rule is that price increases from you are nonnegotiable. Buyers always assume you will negotiate with them. Your position is that you will never negotiate on the price *increase* but you will negotiate on other factors. Your position should be that the prices to your key accounts must go up with all the others at the same time. However, you are prepared to give them a special promotional deal, or rebate, or allowance, or incentive—you can call it what you like—but basically, what you give them is the extra money back for a period of, say, four weeks.

> Tip for sellers raising their prices: *Buyers will always assume price increases are negotiable. Show them your memo from the president telling you they are non-negotiable. (Make sure he sends you such a memo, even if you dictate it yourself.)*

It is very important indeed that you make price increases nonnegotiable to customers. The big ones will always give you a very hard time. They will bureaucratize their power. "Sorry, pal, we have this memo from the main office saying we are not allowed to accept any price increases from suppliers for the next three months." That's very nasty, but it is also a game of bluff. (If they applied this policy to their telephones, or to their electricity, or to new wage agreements negoitated with their trade unions, their telephones would be cut off, their electricity stopped, and their workers would walk out. What does company policy say about that?

That's why you must have an alternative ready. Give them a moratorium on the price increases for a month or even two, but only if they order their usual amount from you. And be certain their invoices carry the new prices from day one, but also show the rebate you have called "special allowance," or some other such elegant phrase. Then it is easier to keep them on the new prices later but to drop the special allowance. The expiration date of the special allowance should be shown on the invoice. Otherwise they'll insist it remain as a discount. Better to make it a credit note if you can, and not show it on the invoice. If they won't play at all on the price increases, then you'll have a lot of trouble. If you are in a strong market position then run a bluff; be happy in the knowledge that most relationships with key accounts last for a long time in practice although the ride can be bumpy. If you are weak, then work harder at it, take care to mix up the deal, give yourself something to negotiate with that they would like to have, but that can be withdrawn if they don't play. I'll keep my fingers crossed for you.

6 Provide sound —and true —explanations

Some companies show their ineptitude when it comes to telling their customers about price increases. Either they are arrogant, or they creep. It is nervousness that does the damage. They are frightened of losing their customers. So they do not put forward their best arguments. Here is the way to do it.

First, add up all the cost increases and show them as percentages against, say, a year ago. Don't fake the figures. The customers will be suspicious enough and they'll spot a lie a mile off. Itemize one or two details (show them a photocopy of your gasoline price per gallon, whatever was your big cost problem a year ago, compared with the gasoline price today).

Demonstrate that the price increase you are imposing is much less than the total of all the cost increases.

How can that come about? Well, now look at your production. You have been making improvements to your process in the past year, haven't you? Your productivity has gone up, hasn't it? You have cleared out some unprofitable parts of your business and invested in new plant. You tell the customers all about your improvements and explain that you should need a lot higher price increase than you are asking for. (Add up the total of the cost increases *without* your productivity savings to arrive at this high figure.) But because you are a sensible company, alive to the needs of your customers, always improving the efficiency of your business, you have been able to absorb a fair amount of those cost increases leaving only the rest to be passed on.

My advice is to look realistically at your figures; look at the improvements you have made to your business. If it were not for these improvements, your customers would be paying a lot more. And that is the literal truth. So why not tell them?

WHEN THE PRICE INCREASE MEANS SURVIVAL, THIS IS WHAT TO DO

In a recession, companies must make price increases in order to survive. The first thing to do is to cut away all the waste, improve the productivity, take the overhead right down to the bare minimum, and run the business as tight as a drum. Now plan your price increases. (Whatever you do, in a recession, do not do it the other way by trying, at first, to recoup your losses from the market through price increases and then taking your cost savings for the difference. That is a sure way to lose your entire business. It is the way of the weak man.)

First, remember to use all the other principles stated here; not too much at one time, not too often; give customers an economy of some kind, look after the big accounts, and provide sound explanations. But all of that might not be enough. Here is what else you must do in order to survive.

First of all, "float" the idea that prices will be going up, but make sure your floated price is higher than the price increase you will require. How you let the trade know is up to you. You offer yourself as a hostage to fortune by doing it, but by not doing so, you are in an even bigger mess. No one promised this would be easy or comfortable.

On no account let your salesmen suggest to the customers that the price increases will be smaller than they actually turn out to be. Salesmen get frightened too, and they must put up with most of the flak from the trade. Some customers will get upset; some will protest. But so far, no one has had to pay the full price increase; at the moment it is all talk. Just talk the market up.

Figure 9.4
Ten ways to increase "prices" without "increasing" prices

1 Revise the discount structure.
2 Change the minimum order size.
3 Charge for delivery and special services.
4 Invoice for repairs on purchased equipment.
5 Charge for engineering, installation, supervision.
6 Make customers pay for overtime required to get out rush orders.
7 Collect interest on overdue accounts.
8 Produce less of the lower margin models in the product line.
9 Write escalator clauses into contracts.
10 Change the physical characteristics of the product.

Figure 9.5
140 ways to ensure your company's survival in bad times

THE GENERAL APPROACH TO SURVIVAL

Look for simultaneous but small changes in costs, sales volume and
    price.
Look for savings in the interactional costs between departments.
Largest savings are gained only in the long term.
Watch the risk to the future of cutting costs today.
Substantial short-term savings can come only from surgical operations.
Concentrate on high-cost areas where substantial savings are to be
    found.
Examine long-standing practices, habits, routines, organizations.

GENERAL MANAGEMENT

Cut salaries and indirect wages.
Cut running expenses.
Cut fixed costs.
Change the organizational structure.
Change the management system and routine.
Evaluate management effectiveness.
Install tight budgeting: to cut marginal expenses; to promote marginal
    opportunities; to create interactive savings.
Install a management audit to appraise: the information; the system and
    control procedures; the organizational structure; the technical and
    management competence.
Buy services from outside: research, product development, data
    processing, accounting, graphics, promotion, sales support, public
    relations, library, information, market statistics, personnel,
    advertising, etc.

PRICING

Plan pricing policy to cover inflation over future years.
Alter pricing methods.
Reduce discounts.
Alter discount structure and method.
Tighten up discount procedure and policy.
Raise prices of small, uneconomic lines.
Charge for services

Figure 9.5 (continued)
140 ways to ensure your company's survival in bad times (continued)

Build inflation clauses into contracts and estimates.
Make price changes to minimize buyer irritation.

FINANCIAL ACCOUNTING

Correct accounts for inflation; watch machinery depreciation, stock
 valuations, land and property valuations, the value of borrowings.
Negotiate better credit terms through purchasing department.
Delay payment to creditors.
Pursue overdue accounts through better control, better
 communications.
Negotiate business terms strictly through your salesmen calling on
 customers' financial controllers.
Speed up cash management by stage payments, rapid banking, flexible
 sources of finance, fast invoicing.
Improve security.
Cut departmental salaries and wages. .
Cut departmental expenses.
Cut departmental fixed costs.
Reduce capital base through use of flexible assets, leasing, bought-out
 services.

MANAGEMENT ACCOUNTING

Replace historical accounting with standard costing.
Question established rule-of-thumb allocations.
Use more flexible costing approach.
Break down variances further.
Faster reconciliation with financial accounts.
Cost products and product groups down to net profit. Cost control
 materials: identify wastage, rejects, breakages.
Allocate factory's indirect costs to products.
Alter stock valuation standards and correct for inflation.
Set labor cost standards closer to realized costs than to ideal.
Identify highly productive labor costs.
Alter transfer pricing systems
Introduce cost accounting to purchasing department, marketing
 department.

Cost the following down to net profit: large orders; customers; markets; depots; sales areas.

PURCHASING

Examine reciprocal trading possibilities.
Identify the company's purchasing Decision Making Unit, examine for weaknesses.
Improve supplier search and evaluation procedure.
Promote purchasing function to contribute to management decisions.
Examine over-specification.
Apply a weighing system to purchases: degree of essentiality of product; level of risk in purchase; proportionate cost against total purchases.
Apply a continuous evaluation of offers.
Concentrate on the high-value materials and components.
Apply regular stock checks.
Apply better quality control on goods inward.
Survey existing suppliers for cost-reduction ideas.
Take discounts for prompt payment.
Negotiate new terms.
Alter product design to allow for standard-parts purchasing.
Improve stock control and reordering system.
Involve purchasing in product elimination decisions.
Place guaranteed orders in exchange for bulk prices.
Improve supplier evaluation for: failure-prevention costs; accident costs; level of service; accuracy.
Use supplier development techniques: in key materials areas; in high-cost areas; in situations of doubtful supply; for unusual demands; for distant suppliers; for nonstandard parts.

PRODUCTION

Check tolerances in specifications and widen.
Check quality control limits and widen.
Limit disruption to work flow.
Reduce prime costs.
Introduce value analysis to examine "use" and "cost" values.

Figure 9.5 (continued)
140 ways to ensure your company's survival in bad times (continued)

Introduce value-analysis engineer to purchasing department.
Introduce value engineering to new product development, and to
    process development.
Reduce labor costs: reducing frequency of performing the task;
    identifying the highly productive tasks; change equipment or
    personnel; eliminate idle time; eliminate overlapping work; eliminate
    duplicate work; eliminate overtime; establish standards of
    performance.
Use less space by condensing operations.
Apply method and work study to activities.
Cut plant and space costs.
Cut indirect salaries and wages, engineering, other services.
Replace fixed costs with flexible costs: use outside services instead of
    high-cost internal services.
Apply job enrichment program to work.
Apply productivity bargaining: incentive schemes, wage structure
    reform, job evaluation, fixed-term contracts, labor flexibility and
    mobility. Change working methods.

THE PRODUCT MIX

Cut high-risk, high-capital projects.
Narrow the range of products.
Make use of short-term and long-term profit opportunities created by
    inflation on existing product range, future product range.
Develop radical new-product ideas to launch when the market demand
    is turning up.
Measure impact of inflation on all aspects of product ranges, supplies,
    labor, distribution, customers, end users.
Develop low-cost, low-risk products.
Develop overseas markets.
Eliminate poor profit producers.
Profit-strip weak products; cut packaging costs; cut sales costs, cut
    stockholding; cut servicing and spare parts; cut promotion and
    advertising; degrade the quality.
Apply promotional resources behind high-profit producers.
Apply promotional resources to products with high overhead
    productivity ratios, high net proftis.
Reduce marginal product innovations.

With price-constrained product, drop it from range and produce one new one above the price and one new one below the price at lower quality.

MARKETING OPERATIONS

Cut advertising costs, particularly advertising production.
Change advertising media mix.
Change advertising appeal.
Reduce sales promotion costs.
Change sales promotions to variable cost (offer incentives per case).
Provide greater flexibility to meet market changes.
Improve market information to identify changes in demand.
Use inexpensive word-of-mouth promotion.
Increase product publicity levels.

SALES OPERATION

Improve sales productivity.
Decrease unprofitable customers.
Concentrate on key accounts.
Develop new high-volume accounts.
Improve customer development activity.
Reduce pre- and after-sales service levels.
Raise volume per order.
Raise order-to-call ratio.
Cut the total sales force size.
Change selling method to cheaper alternative.
Withdraw from uneconomic areas.
Expand into profitable new areas.
Increase number of products per order.
Provide customer incentives.
Introduce sales incentives
Change sales remuneration.
Improve sales training.

Figure 9.5 (continued)
140 ways to ensure your company's survival in bad times (continued)

DISTRIBUTION AND TRANSPORT

Simplify total distribution system.
Reduce distribution points.
Use more central storage, fewer local depots.
Reduce delivery frequency.
Reduce stockholding.
Speed stock flow.
Improve and standardize packaging.
Improve methods and procedures.
Speed up order processing.
Introduce technical improvements, automatic handling.
Change distribution channels.
Reduce storage space.
Use fewer vehicles, larger capacity.
Lengthen life of vehicles.
Reduce maintenance costs.
Use alternative transport methods: road (own vehicles), road (leased vehicles); rail, sea, air.
Introduce collection by customers.

Now at the moment of the price increase, change your business and product policy. Mix it up so that by ordering in a different pattern, customers can get a different discount structure. Rework your discounts at the same time so that if customers order in economic quantities, they can keep their cost increases to the minimum, thus creating maximum savings for you. Drop one or two products from the range. Put new products into the range. Put one or two products down in price. Change the basis of the pricing system. Drop the prices of the basic products but charge for after-sales service, and so on. Introduce a series of cooperative promotional deals for the big customers. Give them a more substantial discount, but for cash up front. I don't know what you can do to change your business, but change it you must. The purpose of the change is not to disguise the fact that your prices are going up by an extraordinary amount, but to offer the customers a different series of options. It puts your salesmen in a negotiating position. When you are weak, then a take-it-or-leave-it policy usually ends up with the customer leaving it. Give yourself room to play. Don't allow the arguments to focus on the principal point of your weakness—your survival price increase.

DECREASING YOUR PRICES

This is an art in its own right. If you want to make money out of decreasing your prices, then you must do two things. You must decrease your prices when everyone else is staying up—stand clear of the forest to be noticed—and you must advertise the price reduction loudly. It is no good just hoping the market will rush to your door just because of your price reduction. Nothing much will happen unless you blast it out to all and sundry. Drop your prices in a big lump—do it once—and do it suddenly, without warning, and put the maximum pressure on the competition. Have *their* key accounts lined up for your salesmen and a secret sales plan for each of your men so they can immediately attack your competitors at their most vulnerable points with your new prices. Go for new, volume business. Pick off your new, targeted customers one by one. Don't expect them to come to you, they won't. Left to themselves, they will go back to their existing suppliers and squeeze them for lower prices with the news of your low prices. You will have to make a strong personal selling effort to win them over. Give your sales force all the backing you can afford. Decreasing your prices is expensive business.

The people most effective at using price reductions to increase business are the supermarket groups. They organize their reduced prices into campaigns. They use suppliers' funds to help them advertise their low prices. And they force suppliers to help them out with special offers and low prices in order to maintain their profit margins during a low-price campaign.

Why don't industrial companies do that? If you are going to lower your prices, then it must be because you want to gain more sales volume or to maintain your existing sales volume. In either case, your suppliers have a vested interest in the objective. So why not use your buying power *before* your price reduction starts to force down the prices of the things you buy? Get them to help you with extra discounts, special free goods, bonus offers, and allowances. If they won't help you, then reduce a little of their sales volume in favor of their competitor who will help you. Then you will have protected your own profit margins to some extent. Why should you have to pay for all the price reductions yourself, when they will get so much of the benefit of extra volume or of the business retained?

For most of you, it will be competition that will force your prices down. You will seldom do it voluntarily. In 1978, merchants and manufacturers of agro-chemical products signed an agreement which effectively stopped merchants from importing chemicals and selling them domestically under foreign labels. As a result, the prices from manufacturers were sustained at a fairly high level, although competition between companies and between merchants was fierce.

Some merchants were left out of the agreement. And large farmers buying in bulk also saw the opportunity to deal with foreign chemical companies directly. Foreign manufacturers and large distributors saw the opportunity to "dump" chemicals on the domestic market at very low prices. Pleas for government intervention resulted in recommendations but no legislation.

Then the cartel broke. Some merchants inside the ring started buying the cheap products when they found themselves losing business. By mid-1981 10% of the market for herbicides went to cheap imports, up from nothing a year before. The multinational companies responded by doing two things. They dropped their domestic prices low in order to protect their volume; secondly they leaned on their foreign subsidiaries to stop dumping and to push up the foreign prices. The foreign subsidiaries did not wish to go along with that policy until the main office made them do so. After all, there is nothing a multinational company manager enjoys doing more than confounding his opposite number in another region, provided that the main office lets him get away with it.

In a multinational company, your biggest rival may not be your closest competitor. He may be the man working in the next office.

USE YOUR PRICE CHANGES TO THEIR MAXIMUM ADVANTAGE

Always have a little price reduction up your sleeve. Your salesman can make use of it to reinforce your reputation for efficiency. Produce a chart showing how expensive the products used to be per unit, how much your productivity has increased and how much you have managed to reduce the prices of your products over the year in "real" terms. Delete the effect of general inflation from the chart, of course, and show you have done so. You will surprise yourself here and there at how good your figures will look.

But always have a little price increase coming up in the future as well. The salesmen can always use it to bring in a little more business a bit faster than it would otherwise come in. Use planned price increases to get customers to stock up.

Don't do it the way in which this travel company whose brochure I am looking at now does it. The brochure says, "If the exchange rate varies before your vacation takes place, then we will advise you of the surcharge." That's a stupid thing to say. Will they give you some money back if the rate gets stronger, do you think? No, all you are going to get from them is a surcharge—windfall losses belong to you, but they'll keep the windfall profits.

Just take care how you present price changes; people are not stupid and you can do yourself untold harm by just concentrating on your need for the extra money without recognizing that you could be giving them an enormous problem at the same time.

SUMMARY

In the long run, all prices will change. Company routines on price changes are not usually thought through well—sometimes blind panic rules the day. A flexible pricing system, with some parts of the range moving up with reasonable frequency, and some parts moving down is the best policy for those companies that can do it. But while it is difficult for companies to move outside their usual industry routine on such things, it is very useful for a company to be able to develop its own pattern of behavior and to get its customers used to it.

Price leadership, like marketing itself, depends on power in the market place. If you are strong, you can carry the market with you. If you are weak, you must make yourself as strong as possible. Develop a unique appeal for your product; sell it for specific purposes in particular market sectors. Then you will carry your price changes and make money. Flexibility is what you need. And if you can gently find a way of bringing your competitors along with you, that is a good idea. If you play a rough game to enforce your price leadership position upon them, you must expect to be challenged sooner or later. And you must be ready to go through with your threats at that time, even if it costs you dearly. The cost of putting out one fire might be very high, but it could save the forest for years to come.

There is no substitute for good, fast market intelligence which is reliable and accurate. Listening to what buyers say about your competitors' prices may be fast, but it will not be reliable, or accurate, and it will not be good. Buyers' unverified information is not the solution to the problem—it may be the problem itself.

If you make a price increase to a buyer who can pass it on to his customers, you will have an easier time than with a buyer who must absorb the cost. If your price increase is higher than the buyer expects, you'll have a hard time. If your price increase is on a product that forms a high proportion of his costs, you'll have a hard time. And you will have a hard time anyway with the big professional buyers who bureaucratize their resistance with memos from directors showing they can't take price increases.

Take your price increases when the market is growing. Take them on selected products where you can. If your competitors are going up, you should go with them, whether you need the extra price or not. Don't hold back. If you want to take advantage of your competitors' price increases, then, at the time they raise their prices, you must put your prices *down*, advertise them, and sell them widely.

Be careful how you construct the letters explaining price increases. Flash warning signals to them, and let them discover later that the price increases are a little lower than they once thought. Mix up your prices, discounts, promotions, to give your salesmen something to negotiate. Look after your top accounts.

If you are going to reduce your prices, announce it to the market with all the funds you can afford; try and retrieve some money from your suppliers if you can. Use your intended price changes as a regular part of your sales story.

*   *   *

Now go back to the start of the chapter and complete the questionnaire again.

Price Negotiation Strategies | 10

CAN YOU SET UP A DEAL?

The more your are committed beforehand to achieving your objectives, the more likely you are to realize them. Answer the questions below. (Comments are on p. 200.)

Q.1 *(a) You have a valuable piece of porcelain for sale. The auctioneer tells you to leave it to him, and he will get the best possible price for it he can. You do not like to agree to that. Why not? (b) You ask him what he thinks it might bring, and he says, "The minimum would probably be about $200." That is better, but not perfect. Why is it not perfect? (c) You ask him what the best possible price is that he has seen an item like yours go for at an auction, and under what conditions. He tells you $450 and describes the conditions. That is better still. Why?*

Q.2 *You are an important politician and your party has just won the election. You and the new President dislike each other and have been rivals for years in the same party. You lead a very important faction of supporters in the party. You are too dangerous for the President to leave loose, and recently you have rallied your supporters behind the President's policies, and have thereby helped to win the election. The President must obviously offer you a job in the Cabinet. You will probably be asked to be in charge of Education or Transportation if the President is to decide. But you want to run Commerce or the Treasury. (Ideally you want to run the Defense or State Department, but you know those jobs will go to the President's close friends and supporters.)*

Your representative meets the President's representative for an informal discussion.

Which job should your representative indicate you are interested in?

(a) Secretary of State or Defense (though you know you won't get them); (b) Secretary of Commerce or the Treasury (the ones you hope to get); (c) leave it to the President as long as it is a big job; (d) no specific job but waiting to hear proposition.

Q.3 *When do you want this informal discussion to take place?*

(a) When the President is considering appointments; (b) before the election campaign starts; (c) on election night; (d) leave it to the President.

Price Negotiation Strategies | 10

One of the largest islands in the Inner Hebrides, off the West Coast of Scotland, has the kind of water on it that is particularly suitable for the manufacture of some of the finest scotch whisky in the world. Scotsmen are particularly grateful to nature for providing them with the resources to manufacture malts on Islay, pronounced "Eyela."

Excise officials are also thankful, for much of their annual funds derive from the duties levied on Islay whisky. The heads of certain distilleries on the island would be equally grateful, were not for the fact that nature has seen fit to put a thirty-mile strip of water between them and the mainland. It is on that strip of water that they find themselves robbed.

Years ago, a nationalized shipping company, Caledonian MacBrayne, had a monopoly on the Tarbert-to-Islay run. The fares were high. The company owned the only ships that could take people to the shore, and they charged up to the limit people could afford. Strangely enough, while charging such high prices, the company also lost money.

Along came a private company to offer them competition. Western Ferries tried out new ideas, and introduced a roll-on/roll-off service. The islanders were delighted. They remarked on the ability of Caledonian MacBrayne to find they could lower their prices all of a sudden. The connection between competition and lower prices was noted over many a product-testing session in the inns.

It is a fact that prices reflect power in the market. If you have sole control over something that people want, you can force them to the limit. But if people have a choice, you are weaker, and they will force down your price. With more competition, there will be many different choices available, some at high price, some at low, and the market will sort them out.

The more you can approach a monopoly situation, the easier it will be for you to obtain your price. In a freely competitive market, this means you must set up the deals properly. You must identify those qualilties of your product or service that are unique to you. You must make people see how important these qualities are. You might also search for customers who do not receive so many competitive offerings.

Unfortunately for the people of Islay, the government stepped in to help its own. When Caledonian MacBrayne lost even more money on the route, instead of making the management attack its costs and sharpen up its business, the company was given a subsidy. Like all government subsidies, this was subscribed to by everybody through their taxes, whether they wanted to subscribe or not. Such is the power of a government monopoly.

The subsidy kept prices so artificially low that Western Ferries lost money also. In 1981, Western Ferries pulled out of the route. As one of the distillers said, with classic understatement, "We await with great anxiety the return to a

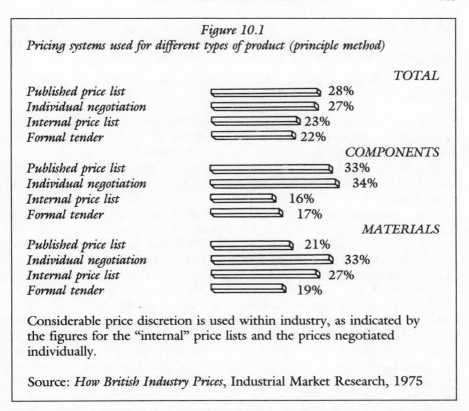

Figure 10.1
Pricing systems used for different types of product (principle method)

TOTAL

Published price list   28%
Individual negotiation   27%
Internal price list   23%
Formal tender   22%

COMPONENTS

Published price list   33%
Individual negotiation   34%
Internal price list   16%
Formal tender   17%

MATERIALS

Published price list   21%
Individual negotiation   33%
Internal price list   27%
Formal tender   19%

Considerable price discretion is used within industry, as indicated by the figures for the "internal" price lists and the prices negotiated individually.

Source: *How British Industry Prices*, Industrial Market Research, 1975

MacBrayne's monopoly." Think about it—there are no prizes for guessing what was going to happen to shipping prices on the Islay route. Incidentally, not only were the prices affected, but the sole shipper reduced the level of service as well. The second largest port on the island no longer receives daily service.

Your business will be concerned with its main customers. Call them national accounts or key accounts or what you will, the fact is that relatively few of them will represent an enormous proportion of your income. If you make profits at the rate of, say, 5% on your sales, then if you can negotiate an extra 1% on the price from all the acounts responsible for half of your total business, you will have increased your total profit by 10%. If you can negotiate a 10% price increase from those key accounts, you will have doubled your total profit.

Consequently, you must pay attention to how you deal with the key accounts—they are all likely to be shrewd and tough buyers who know how to use their power. You must match them in skill.

In setting up the deal, remember that a few things are important all the way through. The first of them could be called *style*. If you are going to deal with a major customer over the years ahead, realize that he will learn how to handle you, just as you will learn how to handle him. If you are too sharp, too tough, too cunning, or simply inefficient, then he will know the next time. So you may get away with something the first time, but he will remember and will seek revenge. The style of approach used on the first deal should establish the relationship for the future.

Note: *The extra profit you chisel on the first deal could cost you a fortune on later ones.*

Suppose that you meet this big prospect for the first time. He might be very aggressive. He might insult you or your company. He might use competition ruthlessly against you, or he might press hard against your weakness. If you give in to this pressure, he will always use the same style on you. So it might even pay you to withdraw from the deal with great courtesy, leaving yourself a way back for later.

If you have the courage to do so, it may mean handsome dividends in the future. If you do business later, he will modify his behavior to you, because he knows now that he cannot browbeat you. Of course, you may lose the deal altogether and never get back in! That is the risk you take. But remember, there is also a risk in staying there and putting up with his pressure, because he will subvert your deals for ever and a day.

Search for *collaboration*, not conflict, is the second point to remember. From time to time, you will get into conflict with your key accounts—a complaint, a clash of will—but if your relationship with them is friendly and cooperative, it can withstand this kind of pressure. At the start, you cannot afford conflict, however, particularly if you are in a strong position. If you use your power brutally, they will either withdraw, or get their own back on the next deal. But to achieve collaboration you will have to sense what they want from you. You will also have to know what you want from them. That means you must explore their situation, find out their background, and assess their needs *before* you make your own presentation. When the buyer says to a salesman right at the start, "Go on then, tell me what you are offering," the classic error of a novice salesman is to respond by doing just that. Instead, he should make the buyer talk about his needs.

Q. *"How much do you charge?"* A. *"How much were you expecting to pay?"*

One of the problems after this initial stage of discovery, is that you don't know how high you can go. You don't know what volume of business to ask for, you might not know what price to ask for. Don't be nervous; if you think you can get it, then ask for it. But test him first. Let him get used to the idea that your price will be high, for example, without actually quoting it. You can suggest it with signals—you can give him an idea of what other people are paying or you can associate yourself with someone else in the market who is known to be expensive. At this stage, don't give him a firm offer. Just test him and watch his reactions. Get him set up to expect a big and important deal—it may not be cheap for him, but the quality of the deal will be just what he needs, and it will therefore be a more effective deal for him than something at low price. To get your price, you must sell the edge of quality between you and your lower price competition. The level at which you pitch your *first offer* is the key to setting up the deal. Perhaps you don't seriously expect to receive it. Perhaps he does not seriously expect to pay it. Perhaps he will make you a counter offer at the other extreme—or, worse still, make you no offer at all, but just say that your price is much too high and you will have to think again. None of that matters. He would behave that way whatever price you quote him. So the rule is, you ask for all that you might possibly get. Because he will work you down, whatever you ask. So you had better start high.

So the general rules are to watch your style and your integrity. If you say something, mean it, and deliver all you promise. Look out for the things he wants from you, and be concerned with the things you want from him. Try and get into a position where, later, you can begin to exchange the two. Ask for all you think you might possibly get. Be brave.

Before you can make the best deal, you will have to find out how strong you are. If you listen to the buyer, he will tell you your prices are too high, your service is not good enough, and he has considerable reservations about your product.

Note: *Buyers can be real pains when they try hard.*

Put all those objections to one side; buyers say all that to test you and to force the maximum concessions from you. Figure 10.2 gives ten points that will help you to assess your strength in dealing with big accounts.

Power depends on the alternatives facing you and the alternatives facing him. If he has hundreds of suppliers chasing him for business, with offers as good as yours, and with products as good as yours, and with prices lower than yours, then you have real trouble. That is a big mountain to climb. He is strong and you are weak. Your prices will go low and there is little you can do about it. On the other hand, if you have so much demand for your product that your factory cannot keep up, you are rationing everyone, and if he does not buy from you and there are plenty of others who will, then you have power. Your prices will go high. If they don't, there is something wrong with your technique.

Revamp these points to suit your particular business. Tighten them up, relate them to particular products. The answers will give you knowledge of your strengths and your weaknesses, and will show you where you have to probe with your questions to him.

Now let us set up the deal in four stages. Define the objectives, what you want. Position the deal in his mind. Get to the first offer. Keep him hooked on your big ideas.

Make a list of all the things you want from him; the total volume of business in all your product groups from all of his sites, over a period of time. This is your uppermost limit; you should get this into his mind. A lot of people play if safe by trying to come in low and then build up later. Don't do it. Go for broke, get the lot early on; you can always come down in your demands, but

Figure 10.2
Ten specific ways to build your bargaining power

PLUS POINTS

Tied to contract already	+5	Sole supply	+5
Have alternative outlet for proposition	+4	Experience of market, customer, negotiation	+4
Degree of uniqueness in proposition	+4	Length of relationship	+3
Access to their multiplicity of decision points, influencers	+3	Amount of information about them	+2
Vital problem for them	+2	Closeness of relationship	+1

And four things to avoid

MINUS POINTS

His links with competition	−3	Far-reaching access to our team	−2
Amount of their information about us, market, experience	−2	Poor history, experience	−2

it is very difficult to go up. Generally if you start small, you'll stay small. If he is single sourcing his supplies, don't ask him to double source and split the business with you. You can always settle on this later if you have to. Ask him for the lot—in this world if you don't ask, you'll never know, so go for your top limit. The chances are you will not get it all, so be prepared. Divide your uppermost limit into those things you want badly—your "must have" limit— and the other things you can put into your "like to have" category. The "must have" things cover the deal you expect to do; you are going to struggle like mad before you settle for less than this.

In setting your objectives, you must also know the point at which you will walk out. When you walk out you will do it nicely, with grace and charm, and you will leave yourself a way back. But you must know in advance where your bottom line is. Whatever you do, though, don't get hooked on it in your mind. If you concentrate upon that figure, they can hit you with some unexpected threat, make you frightened of losing the business, and then make you an offer just above your bottom limit. People get bulldozed into saying yes and then accept bad deals.

> Remember: *Don't let him bulldoze you; practice saying "no." You can change your mind and say "yes" later. What's all the hurry?*

Of course, they are setting up the deal with you, too. First they are going to give you the impression that you cannot have their business at all. They'll make you work hard, to see how eager you are. They'll ease up a bit later, giving you the hope of saving something—but only if the price is right.

So get your objectives sorted out and hold on to them: your top one, your expected one, and the bottom line. And if you settle for the bottom line, call it "failure"—after all, it is next to not getting the business at all. Don't persuade yourself it is success just because you landed a piece of business at any price.

Now there is a problem, because if you go in too high, too soon and stick to those early big demands, and if they are thinking of something much less, they will be offended or frightened and will walk away. If you've been too strong, you will lose them. If you don't know how they are going to react to what you want, don't make an explicit demand; rather suggest it instead. Get the idea floated in their minds. Talk about the deals done elsewhere. Reassure them that this is a perfectly normal deal for them. And give them a little time to get used to your idea if they are not expecting it. One good technique is to ask them not to make up their minds now, but to think about it first and sleep on it. Some quite big ideas need to be mulled over; tell them this, it is quite true. You can use the technique even in the same meeting. Get the big idea out into the open and say you would like to discuss this with them, but not now— a bit later. That will allow time for the idea to take shape in their minds without setting them against you. If you hit them with a big idea, and ask for an immediate decision, they will say no and you will have the devil of a time unseating them.

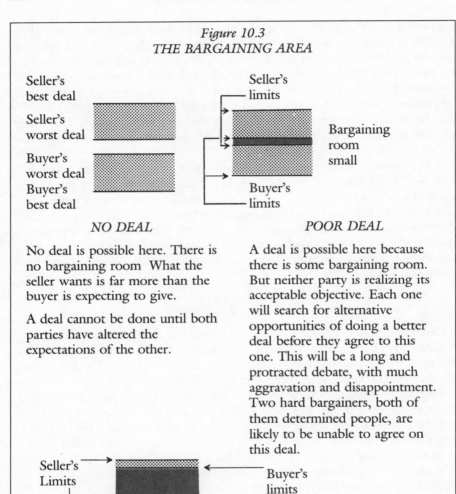

Figure 10.3
THE BARGAINING AREA

NO DEAL

No deal is possible here. There is no bargaining room What the seller wants is far more than the buyer is expecting to give.

A deal cannot be done until both parties have altered the expectations of the other.

POOR DEAL

A deal is possible here because there is some bargaining room. But neither party is realizing its acceptable objective. Each one will search for alternative opportunities of doing a better deal before they agree to this one. This will be a long and protracted debate, with much aggravation and disappointment. Two hard bargainers, both of them determined people, are likely to be unable to agree on this deal.

A GOOD DEAL

Here a successful deal is entirely possible. Both parties can get most of what they want from it, little clash is likely; disruption will be caused only by a personality clash or by bad communications between the bargainers.

Finally, keep a key account hooked on to your big ideas. Give them reassurance that although the idea may appear big it is quite normal. Keep in contact with them—if they walk away and mean it, you will have to go after them. In that case, ask them for their counterproposal, make them bring their own ideas out into the open. Find a way to be persistent, nicely, firmly. For example, suppose you are selling industrial adhesives, used in their production process. However good you are, you will not get a big order immediately because the products must be tested extensively in their process. Most industrial adhesives salesmen will settle for selling a sample for testing. Once the test has been run, and if it works, then they haggle for the business. This cannot be right. Half the time the test is badly controlled, and they mess up the results themselves. Or the results in terms of performance are inconclusive. At best, the customer decides to split his order with his existing supplier and the new one picks up a small slice of the business.

The deal has not been established properly. The salesman should agree to supply the test sample only if there is agreement with the customer about volume, price and supply, assuming the test to be successful. Once the customer knows that the test is important, because he sees the product as replacing his existing product, then he will take more care to inform people about the test; he will take more care over the test; he will also presell his own colleagues upon the implications of a successful result. In other words, he is already buying in his mind and is looking for the test to confirm the decision. Also, because large volume is now involved, the salesman himself will take extra care to monitor the test and to work with the important technical personnel.

Finally, if you want to keep him hooked on your ideas, you should make friends with the important decision-makers in his business. You should help them to solve problems—don't go overboard; you can do everything to excess. But once they start to rely on you, you are most of the way there.

Avoid a deadlock if you can—but you may have to bring things to a deadlock early on in the process to force them to come to terms. It is a rare circumstance. Don't let the late stages of the discussion get deadlocked—reason and logic will fly out the window as emotion develops.

FOREIGN EXCHANGE

In 1976 the author agreed to lead a management seminar in Jakarta on the basis of a fee per head for each person attending. For some reason, which remains a mystery, the deal was quoted in the Indonesian currency, the rupiah. The author should certainly have known better than to make such a mistake. Before the seminar was run, the Indonesian government devalued the rupiah by no less than 36%! The effect, of course, was to lose apparently one-third of the revenue by the time the money was converted.

If you have to price deals in different currencies, there is a fairly simple rule to follow, provided you have the choice. Price them in the stronger currency of the two. That will put the odds in your favor. If you have a choice of pricing in sterling or lire, choose sterling. Or if your choice lies between sterling or D Marks, choose D Marks. If it is between sterling and the U.S. dollars, you are on your own. (For me, I would pick sterling in the long run because of the North Sea Oil—but then look at the mistakes I make!)

Actually, the paradox of the Indonesian deal was this. When the local organization came to the managers in Jakarta to price the deal, they took the proposed fee per head and used their standard cost-accounting system to arrive at their selling price. They multiplied the author's fee by three. As a result, the Jakarta managers were surprised to be invited to attend an international seminar that was so inexpensive. They turned up in hordes. We had nearly 200 of them. The deal turned out to be better for the author and better for the organizers also.

Despite the fact that this example appears to prove the case for penetration pricing, and the case for prices being based upon standard costs, I maintain this was a "rogue" result. For every occasion it turned out to be a success, there were 100 failures. But it might be nice to know that it is possible to do nearly everything wrong and still be successful. (It is equally possible to fail when doing nearly everything right.)

PROGRESS PAYMENTS

Your price will have a different value to you depending on when you get paid. If you were given $1,000 in a year's time, it would be worth much less than were it given to you now. For example, if you were paid now, you could bank the money and earn perhaps 10% or more on it, making it worth $1,100 in a year. And inflation will damage the value of money you receive in the future.

So your price must be fixed up with your terms. If you have a long manufacturing lead time, or if you are going to incur heavy costs at the beginning of the contract, but it will not be completed for a long time, it could pay you to devise a system of progress payments. It is common with many construction projects to ask for one-third payment at the start, one-third during and one-third on completion. The system could be applied in many other money-intensive projects. Another way of solving the financial problem is to ask the customer to pay for the costs of the materials himself and to pay you just for working on them. If cash flow is your problem, then think creatively about how you set your terms on large orders.

It's management's job to get the salesman in there with a fighting chance. There's only so much a salesman can do on his own. He can have considerable impact on the results of the business by the sheer skill which he demonstrates in negotiating big deals, and by his vigor and intelligence, but whatever he is offering must be within reach of the competitor's quality and price, and preferably better in one or the other.

The salesman's personal posture must be strong too. He must be seen to be important. He must be welcomed by the buyer. The power at his elbow is determined by the product or service he has to offer, and his strength in the marketplace. If everybody wants it, he is strong; it it outguns the competition, he is strong; if it is reasonably priced, though at a premium perhaps, he has a fighting chance of winning the business.

It's management's job to get him there with the right products, the right prices and the right policies that are within reach of the competition. To send the salesman into a desperate selling situation where his product is nowhere near as good as the competition, or is massively overpriced, or outdiscounted, will leave the salesman working on his wits alone. This leads to bad deals, customer complaints and a high personnel turnover in the sales force. Ultimately it leads to bankruptcy.

QUICK DEALS ARE BAD DEALS FOR SOMEONE

If you need the business very badly, then your quick deals will be bad deals. Whatever you do, give yourself time to play and think—as much time as possible. If you are in a desperate situation, don't reveal it to the other party. If you are facing a financial crisis, it will call upon all your skill, flair and self-confidence to dig yourself out appropriately. Fight your way out of it carefully and selectively. Do not be panicked into making any deal quickly if you can possibly avoid it.

You've got to be able to afford to pass up a bad deal. Careful calculation, hard work and another four hours on top of the average working day, will often turn a poor situation around.

SUMMARY

Summarizing the situation we can say this: the style you use at the first meeting with our national account will carry you through for a long time. They learn how to handle you; if you are seen to be weak and indecisive, then they react by putting pressure on you. If you are aggressive, then this will draw a counterattack. You need a firm, confident and pleasant manner, and you should be seen to be able to deliver your promises.

Establish your edge over the competition and make your customer want it. That's what will get you the price you want in the end. If you can set up alternative customers for what you have to offer, it will strengthen your hand. Don't use the threat of them ruthlessly, but have them in case they are needed. Principally it improves your confidence.

You are not in the industrial relations field, so you can avoid conflict bargaining. Later in the relationship, when both parties know each other well and have been doing business for some time, some conflict is inevitable. But avoid it early on, or when you are in a tricky persuasive situation. Your first offer is the key to the size of the deal. Actually, you should get them to make the first offer to you if you can (see the next chapter). Make out a list beforehand of all that you want from the customer and test it in your questions to him. Go for all of the business you want, and don't let him drag you down to your bottom limit. On the other hand, you always have the right to walk out if his demands are too steep, so know the point of departure before you start walking.

Float your big ideas, and give buyers time to think about them. Keep at it, don't let them drag you away or make up their minds against you. They'll take you down if they can. It's your job to set the up high and keep them there. Price your overseas deals in the stronger currency.

Price Presentation | 11

Before reading the chapter, complete the answers to these questions They are designed to make you think about price presentation. (Comments are on p. 201).

HOW SHARP A PRICE PRESENTER ARE YOU?

Q.1   *(a) As a seller:*
Write down your company's sales here ($'s)   _____(a)
(Or your division, or product you are responsible for) Write
it out again but this time take off the last two figures (i.e.
divide it by 100)   _____(b)
Write down your net profit ($'s)   _____(c)
Call the figure (c) 100%. When the figure (b) is compared
to it, what is its percentage?   _____%(d)
   Now just look at your figure (d). This is the increased percentage of profit you could achieve, if you were able to negotiate all your selling prices at 1% more than you currently achieve.
   Or you would achieve the same result if you were able to negotiate all your discounts down by 1%?
   Buyers can do the same exercise. 1% saved on all their purchases can easily mean an increase in net profit of 10% or more in a manufacturing business.
   We can take it that price bargaining has an important and direct impact upon profitability. Remember the first rule of bargaining. If you don't have to bargain, don't.

Q.2   *In a seminar, one-half the audience is asked to sell car license plates to the other half of the audience. Each buyer is told he must buy one and only one plate and is given a maximum budget of $1,000. Each salesman is told he must sell. There is a time limit of four minutes. Here are the license plates: how much do you think each one brings on an average? (The prices vary over different seminars, no salesman knows what price the other salesmen are asking, and there is very little competitive bidding between buyers.)*

(a)	*RU1*	*Your guess*	$_____
(b)	*HIM 1*	*Your guess*	$_____
(c)	*MDX 227*	*Your guess*	$_____
(d)	*IAM 007*	*Your guess*	$_____
(e)	*RU 12*	*Your guess*	$_____
(f)	*HIM 123*	*Your guess*	$_____
(g)	*RU 123*	*Your guess*	$_____
(h)	*HIM 12*	*Your guess*	$_____

153

Q.3 *You have submitted a quotation of $2,500 to this householder for double glazing his six main windows. He shows you competitive quotations of $2,100 and $2,900 and asks you to justify your price. Write in how you would make use of the following price-bargaining techniques. (Write in the specific things you would say.)*

(a) *Which of the two competitors would you call his attention to in terms of price, and how would you express it?*

_____

_____

(b) *He talks about the lower priced competitor. How do you handle this?*

_____

_____

(c) *How would you show a small unit price?*_____

_____

(d) *How could you spread the price thin?*_____

_____

(e) *How could you miniaturize price differences?*_____

_____

(f) *What equivalent spending could you demonstrate?*_____

_____

(g) *What are the cost penalties of not buying?*_____

_____

Price Presentation | 11

Studying the four thousand words in this chapter can make you more money than any investment you have ever made in the stock market. Over the years, a decent gilt-edged investment will pull back interest and capital gain for you just below the level of inflation. Check your savings accounts, your endowment policies, your shares in public companies or unit trusts over the past ten years, to see if this is true. So investments like those are a sure way to lose money. It is much better to invest in your skill. Your skill at price presentation can earn you huge rewards, and here is an inside tip—most people are bad at it.

> Question for investors: *Why put your money into a savings account when inflation will wash away the value of your savings? Why not invest in your own skill?*

The first thing to realize about price presentation is that it is painful for the buyer to think about it. He gets very excited, we hope, at what you are going to give him—your product, your service, the benefits you offer him. He gets gloomy at the thought of what he has to give in exchange, the price. So you must ease him through the pain barrier, give him an aspirin.

Whether they say anything about it or not, buyers will always think long and hard about your price. Some of them may be quite nice to you, but privately may think they can do better elsewhere. Others will give you a hard time. A really professional buyer will give you a hard time anyway, even when he has made up his mind to buy from you. The thing to remember is to try to get buyers into a position where they believe they are going to buy from you, before the price issue is raised. In other words, get them thinking about what you are going to give them, before they think of what they are going to have to pay you.

Throughout the presentation of your pricing story, you must be in total control, unafraid and confident. That part of your deal should be rehearsed over and over again until the ideal method has been evolved.

EIGHT GUIDELINES TO FOLLOW

1 Keep your price until the end
Make sure the buyer is excited about what you can offer him before telling him

155

the price. If he opens with, "Tell me what it will cost me," say you will, and then go on asking him questions about his business. There are rare times when you might open with your price. When a retailer telephones a National Cash Register sales office to inquire about a new machine, a salesperson asks him early on if he knows what the price is likely to be. This is to flush out those without money and to get the deal set up properly. The sales team for Nescafé in Sweden opens with a phrase such as: "I would like to tell you why you should buy the most expensive instant coffee in the country, Nescafé." They are also setting up their deal. Premium-priced suppliers might go in with an early line like this, to set up the deal, but they are exceptions to the rule which says: "Keep your price until the end." If you offer the lowest price in the market, don't lead with it unless the prospect is completely satisfied about the quality. And even then it is best to sell the benefits first, and to let your low price help you clinch the deal. A buyer will suspect you are proposing to sell him rubbish if you focus on the price alone.

2 Make him open, if you can
You will have an edge if you can get him to suggest what he might be prepared to pay for your product. Then you know the limit of what he expects, and you are free to turn down his bid and move your response to the other end of the scale. "How much are you paying now?" you might ask. "What's your present cost?" "What do you expect to pay?" With persistence, sellers can often determine the other party's ideas on price. "How much will you charge me for writing this 4,000 word article?" says the magazine editor to you. "What are your usual rates for your top contributors?" must be your reply. Whatever he quotes now, you should indicate that you were expecting something more. Then be silent and let him answer.

There may be occasions when you want to get your blow in first before he

---

Figure 11.1
Seven guidelines for price presenters

Keep your price until the end.

Make him open, if you can.

Make him do the work.

Sandwich your price between benefits.

The price should be non-negotiable.

Show him the penalties of not buying.

Don't squeeze too hard against weakness.

has a chance to think about it and give you a very low figure. But usually you'll find a small advantage if you can get him to open.

3 Make the buyer work hard

If he objects to your price, ask him to explain why. Ask him what he thinks the price should be. Ask if he knows how much more than that he could be paying. Ask him to justify his demands. Don't do this aggressively; ask casually and nicely. Don't argue, but make him do the work.

4 Sandwich your price between benefits

Price is nasty for him. So cover it with something nice. Some people teach you to name your price and then keep quiet. That, in my view, is wrong. Certainly don't deliver a long monologue after you name your price, but sweeten it up a bit by reminding him of one of the benefits included in the price. "It's going to cost $25, but that includes the tax and free delivery to your office." Then stop.

5 Try to make your price non-negotiable

Don't let him pressure you by indicating that he knows you will come down on your opening bid, because, as he says, everyone else does. He is testing to see if you are serious about your price, to find out whether you are floating a figure. Respond immediately by telling him it is unlikely you can reduce your initial figure. Don't give him an early indication that you are willing to deal. That can always come later.

6 The cost penalties of not buying

Always have in the back of your mind what he will lose if he does not buy from you. Add up the value of your benefits to him—if he refuses to buy, he will lose them. You can often hold him at the bargaining table by using these figures gently. Don't threaten him; but there is nothing to stop you from working out the calculations for your own benefit (but out loud so he can hear you).

7 Don't squeeze too hard against weakness

Remember, you will probably have to meet this man and do business with him again. You want to be able to look him straight in the eye when you do. And you want to face a man who continues to trust you. So, in a deal, if you happen to have him over a barrel, if he is desperate to get what you offer at any price, then don't take him to the extreme. Show him how far you might go with your price but then ease up a bit. If you squeeze hard against extreme weakness, he'll get his own back the next time around.

8 Let him win something

Always give him a good fight if he argues with you over your price. He will appreciate you more; he will respect you more. But don't lord it over him, even if you have won. Give in on something toward the end; it might be something small, it might even be something you were saving up for him all the time; but let him win it from you. You'll make a friend and not an enemy.

HANDLING PRICE RESISTANCE

He likes receiving benefits from you. But he resents giving you something in exchange, such as money. He is going to argue over it. He is going to see if he can get your price down. So he is going to resist you. Not all of the time, of course; in very many deals, the price is taken as read, with little argument. If you buy this book at a bookstore, you will not argue over the price. But if you buy 20 copies for your management team and executives, you will try to buy it at a discount.

First rule of buying: *Find out how much discretion the salesman has.*

Price objections fall into three broad categories, and it is important to have a ready technique that suits you and your product to deal with each type of objection. The most common resistance is competitive—somewhere, someone is cheaper than you. The next type of resistance is different: The buyer says he cannot afford to buy, he has no money in his piggy bank. The last type of objection concerns the idea of "value" for money. He feels that what you are offering is too expensive and is not worth the price you are asking.

Second rule of buying: *If the salesman has any discretion, then get it from him.*

The responses to the three types of price resistance are all quite different. Study those responses, work on one or two in each category, and try them out in your price presentation. Rehearsal, practice and the use of imagination will pay great dividends, and will get you through many a price-pain barrier.

RESISTANCE: WE HAVEN'T GOT THE MONEY. WE CANNOT AFFORD IT. WE HAVE NOTHING LEFT IN OUR BUDGET.

With this type of objection, it is necessary to do two things. The first is to explore their position thoroughly on these matters before quoting the price. The second is to establish the fact that they would buy, wouldn't they, if only they did have enough money, have the budget available, or whatever.

Probe the cash position
Early on, if you suspect that this kind of objection might be raised later, ask them questions relating to their cash flow in the business. Find out if they are doing better than expected; if they are profitable. Calculate the amount of money they must find for your products and see if this is a large sum or a small sum to them. This probing will reveal openings that you can use later if they say they cannot afford your product.

Probe their budget
Sometimes they will say they have no budget just to put you off. It's the handiest excuse they have available. First, respond by saying, "If you did have the budget available, what would be your reaction?" If they are giving you an excuse, this will flush it out; otherwise you can isolate the budget question as the only objection and then deal with it. Next, find out when their new budget period will start.

Find out when they must start ordering things to fit into their new budget period. Then demonstrate that your terms of payment are such that if you take an order for delivery on a particular date, the payment will fall due in their new budget period. Sometimes there is another budget somewhere else upon which they can draw. Sometimes, also, if you demonstrate there are cost savings to be made with your product, you can see whoever is in charge of setting the budgets, demonstrate your case and break the budget limit this way. Their budget statement needs deep probing. If they want your product badly enough, they will find a way around the problem. Or else you might need to find someone more senior who can find the way.

> Third rule of buying: *If the salesman hasn't got enough discretion, get to his manager, because he has more authority to give you money.*

Sell the terms or payments
Get him off the price and sell the terms instead. Show him how favorable the payment terms are. A cigarette salesman shows his customers how they can use the credit offered by his company to supply some of the working capital they need for their business. If they turn their cigarette stock every week and get 30 days credit, then the cigarette company is helping them finance their business. If you can stage the payments, or give extended credit, then sell those things hard—not the price.

Spread your price thin
Don't highlight a big unit price—cut it up into thin bits. It would be much easier to sell this book if we could point out, sensibly, that for all this management information and advice leading possibly to substantially increased profits for the reader, the cost is merely eighteen cents a page. It is possible to make it sound really ridiculous by saying the price is only three cents for every forty words. A little creative ingenuity is called for in spreading the price thin, but without making it sound stupid.

A salesman for poultry vaccine showed that the cost of preventing the flock from getting a terrible disease would be only "one egg per bird." To a poultry farmer, that sounds a good deal cheaper than the $50,000 he might lose if he did not vaccinate his flock.

Show that the price is a small part of his cost
If you sell coatings of high quality, you might charge $5 a part for a standard

application on a customer's component. But if the component is used in vehicle manufacture, the cost of making the part itself might be $5. As a proportion of the customer's total cost, the cost of the coating then is high—very high. You can expect a great deal of pressure on price. But if the same $5 coating is applied to a component used in the aerospace industry, then the total part cost might be $50. In this case, it is not the cost of the coating that will attract the resistance—it is the speed of the turnaround of the service. Because the costs of parts are so high, they must be moved quickly, otherwise there will be high interest charges. So there will be less argument on price. Probe what proportion of your customer's total cost will be represented by your product, and it might provide an opening for you.

RESISTANCE: YOUR COMPETITORS ARE CHEAPER. IT'S MORE THAN WE ARE PAYING NOW. WE CAN DO BETTER THAN THAT.

Never be afraid of competition if your product is higher priced. Be proud of it. Find out why you are more expensive; find out all you can about what your product or service will do that the competitor's won't.

Find out about a competitor who is known to be even higher in price than you—and also find out where your product has benefits over his. Now you are equipped to deal with this resistance. Competitive knowledge is the name of the game and there is no substitute for it. Most salesmen lose because they don't know what they are up against.

A clever buyer will always tell you he can buy cheaper elsewhere. What he won't tell you is that their product is no good, their service is no good, and that he has no intention of using them.

Compare yourself with higher priced competition
When he takes you down to a lower priced competitor, you take him up to a higher priced one. When he argues low, you argue high. You'll split the difference around the middle. Whose price is that? Yours.

Show the savings your product makes
It's not the price that is important, it is what the product does for him. It promises a more efficient production. It saves him time. It is more convenient. It is more reliable. The service is better. The disadvantages of not having such things can be costed: What is the cost to him of a breakdown due to a faulty product? He is paying for your reliability. Ask him when the last breakdown was and if it was serious. If you can show him the possible cost of not doing business with you, you will overcome the little extra he must pay.

Show reason for the difference
If he thinks your product is simply overpriced, then you should show him *why*

Figure 11.2
Meeting objections to your price

WHEN HE SAYS	YOU SAY
He doesn't have the money	What's his budget? What's his cash? Look at your terms He will actually *save* money Your cost is a small part of his total cost What is he spending now?
Your competitors are cheaper	Some are more expensive. But look at the cost savings to him Show the reason for the difference Compare product differences Miniaturize price differences
It's not worth it. *You are charging too much*	How much is too much? Everyone pays the same Look at the returns to him from your offer The unit price is very small What else would they spend their money on? But look at the discount they will receive

---

yours is more expensive. Without giving him a cost breakdown—bad thing to do—give him an example of the extra-special effort you put into quality control, or materials, or whatever. Such a gambit is not very strong; it is only a feature, but it helps a bit. It helps to justify your price from a moral point of view.

Compare the product difference to the price difference
This is the standard method, and highly effective. It is based on knowing your product and knowing your competitor's product. A fleet-car salesman for Chev-

rolet may meet a Ford fleet customer. He may want to sell him an upgraded Caprice against the existing Ford Fairmount. He will call for a product comparison from his main office. He will then take each item and point out the differences between the two models.

Using this technique, the seller should first of all isolate the price *difference* between the two products (not the whole price of the unit). That already makes the argument look quite small. One $60,000 earthmoving machine may be $1,000 more expensive than a competitor's. The salesman should argue for the $1,000, not the $60,000.

Then take the competitor's specifications and show carefully and slowly, point by point, how the two specifications compare and where you have advantages. Don't hurry it. Make the buyer see every point, and agree to it before moving on to the next. If you do it properly and your products are good, you'll get your price. Show the differences in your products in terms of the advantages *to* the buyer, not just in terms of the rival features.

Miniaturize the price difference

Once the price differences are established, make them small. After all, if the earthmoving machine costing $1,000 extra is going to last seven years, then that is only about $140 a year extra on the price. As a matter of fact, the extra cost is only a few cents a day every day the machine is used. That's nothing compared to the advantages. Take the difference, and make it small. Be ingenious and creative.

RESISTANCE: YOU ARE CHARGING TOO MUCH. IT'S NOT WORTH IT. HOW CAN YOU CHARGE THAT?

With a premium-priced product toward the top end of the market it is possible to find customers who are used to paying a lot less. Their expectations are low— they accept your high quality and most of your arguments, but they think you are overcharging. Their objections may be almost on moral grounds. The truth is these customers are generally not in your league and have to be educated up to your prices. A woman who is used to spending $8 on having her hair done by the best hairdresser in town, would be likely to object when confronted by a salon charge of $40 for the same thing.

One good principle before you start is to signal the high price early on. Don't quote it firmly too soon—otherwise they'll rush away—but don't let them get a nasty shock. Warn them throughout your presentation that this qualilty is the top, but it has to be paid for. They'll get the message.

Everyone pays the same

You must reassure them nicely that they themselves are not being singled out for especially high charges. Being able to demonstrate that everyone pays the

same is very useful. Don't put them down if they complain about your price—
make it clear you understand this, and they need not worry because they will
get top value for the price.

Show the returns from your offer

Get into their production process and demonstrate the savings that your product
can make for them. Concentrate on those savings. Calculate the gross over the
life of the product. Present them as extra profits. Compare those extra profits
over time with the small amount of extra cost which they have to pay now.

Show how small the unit price is

By the time they take your quotation and break it down into the chunks of
product they use, the cost per chunk will look quite small. They don't price
gold on the basis of a kilo bar, have you noticed? That way investors would
think of having to spend $25,000 on bullion. No, it is priced per ounce. Makes
it much easier to bring in gold investors, small and large alike, when they are
thinking of spending only $500 or so at a time.

Show what else they could spend their money on

If you can show them how much they are spending with you, then you can
demonstrate that they are spending that kind of money on something else
without even thinking about it. Sending a man on a training course costing
$75 a day can be seen to cost them only the equivalent of one day of his salary
and overhead—or the equivalent of two days' subsistence at a decent hotel.
Putting in a small computer costing $10,000 is less than the cost of an accounts
clerk. The cost of putting $25,000 of safety equipment into their production
process which will last over five years, is less than the cost of the coffee machine
subsidy for the office girls, fifty postage stamps a day or eight packets of cigarettes. Be creative. Such comparisons last in their imagination.

Sell the discounts

Never mind the price, look at the discount. If this is your case, then make it
strongly. If your discounts are bigger than your competitor's discounts, even if
your list price or your net price is higher than the competition's, then concentrate
on the discounts. It will not be difficult. Most buyers are more excited about
getting an extra, large discount than they are about getting a lower unit price.
In that case, don't quote the "everyone gets the same" argument. Leave him to
enjoy the thought that he has won the extra discount himself. It will pay dividends.

Figure 11.3
Quotations include things other than price

CHECKLIST OF MECHANICAL POSSIBILITIES.

Whether prices are negotiated, estimated, or contracted for, they might include specific provisions for the following:

Relation to List Prices

Net price quotations to distributor
Less discount to distributor

Provision for Resale Prices

Suggested prices
Recommended resale prices
Advertised resale prices

Pricing Extras, Replacement Parts and Repairs

Separate charges
Inclusive with original purchase or with main product

Discount Structure

Cash (for quick payment of invoices)
Quantity (for large purchases)
Trade (for being at certain level in distribution process)
Promotional (e.g., co-op advertising)

Delivery/Transportation

Prepaid or C.O.D.
Base point (i.e. prices are calculated from a specified point,
    regardless of where shipment originated)
Cost of insurance and freight (C.I.F.)
F.O.B. Factory (Free On Board)—buyers pays cost of transporation
    to his location, plus the same base price paid
    by all other buyers
F.O.B. Destination—seller pays cost of transportation to buyer's
    location
Freight equalization—distant buyer is quoted a delivered price
    consisting of F.O.B. factory price, plus delivery charges
    from location closest to customer.
Delivery included.

Other Items Affecting Quoting

Guarantee and warranty service
Installation charges
Service/maintenance charges
Allowances (e.g., promotional, co-op advertising)

QUOTATIONS

Most companies offer quotations badly—very badly. What they commonly do is to list all the specified features of their offer, add a quantity and then show a price. On the back they show the company's terms of business.

At one crack, and with one piece of paper (often tucked inside a skimpy plastic cover) they throw away all the salesman's training, all the careful rehearsal of benefits, all the image building of the company's advertising and public relations and, instead, focus the buyer's attention on the one thing they want to get him away from—the price. Some companies' quotations are mind boggling in the stupidity of their presentation.

The last thing you want to do is focus a buyer on the wretched price—you want to get him excited about the benefits. So you must sell the benefits to him in the document. The price is the thing he must give to you, within the terms you outline—but the reason why he will buy is because of *what you will give him*.

Company literature is not sufficient to convey the benefits, because literature, by its nature, must generalize. It is too long, and it is not specific.

This is what you should do. First, make certain everything about the presentation of your quotation is of high quality. It must be readable, it must be well typed and laid out, it must be presented as if it is very valuable. Ten dollars spent on a handsome grained binder with your company emblem engraved on it, will be money well spent. Have one top-quality binder made up with your quotation, only one to make it rare, and if you have to submit copies, they can go into ordinary covers. But have the top-quality binder sent to the senior executive of the customer's company.

Next, type out a simple contents page, give the quotation a title and a date. Make sure your salesmen do not promise a customer they will receive a quotation quickly, when in fact it will take some time to prepare. Always be sure the quotation arrives on their desk earlier than they expect it. In other words, teach your salesmen to promise delivery of the quotation by a specific date, well ahead, knowing perfectly well that you will be able to beat it. In that way, they will see you are an efficient company because you even *beat* your own promises. (If salesmen promise a date too early, the prospect thinks your service is poor if you are a day late.)

In the quotation, use a page or two to draw up an outline of the customer's problem you are trying to resolve. This is taken from the notes the salesman has taken at the meetings, hopefully, or the survey you have completed. Summarize what the customer's problem is. Then show the objectives of your proposition and specifically how they meet the customer's requirements. Here you are listing the *benefits* to him of your proposition, not the features you build in. Then run a page analyzing, if you can, the cost benefit of accepting your proposition as against any alternatives he might be considering.

Don't name competitors specifically, but make general assumptions. Show him how big his benefits are when added up over a period of time. Show him how small his unit costs are.

Indicate the distinctive characteristics of your proposition which the competition cannot afford, prove them with figures, or by any other means.

Then, and only then, show him the page with your specification and your price. Show in your price how it breaks down into a small, unit cost, and also show, after the price, what it includes in the way of service.

Then quote your terms and add one final benefit.

Finally, include your company literature in all its glory in a pocket of the binder.

You are not guaranteed to win all the quotations you submit with this method, but you will win more than you would otherwise, were you to do it any other way.

Figure 11.4
Tailor make your quotations

High-quality binder, well-typed proposal

Deliver quote *earlier* than you promised

Outline his problem

Show your proposed objectives

Show your proposition

Show your benefits

Show cost analysis versus his savings

Show your unique qualities

Show specification, price, terms

Summarize

SUMMARY

On price be prepared. There is no substitute for knowing the market, and knowing the competition. Calculate the benefits you give the other party. Calculate, in particular, the things you offer (including your own personal advice and skill) that your competitors do not, and then force them into the buyer's mind. When he argues over your price, those are the things you can use to hold him. Calculate all the other little ways you can ease him through the price-pain barrier—through payment terms, through discounts, through extra services just for him. Be honest; but you can put your prices in the best light by showing him that the competition is more costly in the long run, that he is spending this kind of money on other things, that your extra quality justifies the extra cost, that he is not being overcharged.

Be creative and imaginative with your price presentation. Don't be afraid of high price, be proud of it. Use your high price to make your high-quality argument for you. Don't be defensive about price—he will rarely buy the cheapest in the market, so someone has to win with a higher price. It could be you. If he wants you, he'll pay.

Price Bargaining Tactics | 12

Before reading the chapter, complete the answers to these questions in the spaces on the left-hand side. Then without looking at the answers, read the chapter. Finally, complete the answers again, making any changes you think fit. Score both sets of your answers This tells you how much the chapter has affected your opinion. Scores are at the end of the book (p. 203).

HOW GOOD A BUYER ARE YOU?

Imagine you are a very devious buyer. You want the best deal for your company. You must stay within the law; you must maintain your integrity if you have to work with this seller again; you must not tell lies; your deals must stick. But you want the best possible deal each time.

Q.1   *You want to book one major hotel for a conference package. What do you do first?*

(a) Telephone their reception to ask for the conference-room rate; (b) ask their banquet sales manager to come and see you; (c) write and ask them for their best terms, laying out what you want; (d) talk to rival hotel banquet sales managers first; (e) tell them the booking will be for about 100 people (but you know it will be for only 50 in the end)?

Score   **Score**

___   ___

Before reading chapter.   After reading chapter.

___   ___

Q.2   *In seeking competitive information from other hotels, is your manner and conversation:*

(a) warm and friendly; (b) assertive; (c) offhand; (d) concentrated solely on price?

Score   **Score**

___   ___

Before reading chapter.   After reading chapter.

___   ___

Q.3   *Now that you know what the competitors can offer, you can approach your chosen hotel to see what deal can be made. You have practically made up your mind to give them the business, but you want the best deal from them.*

(a) Do you open first and tell them the business is theirs if their price is right; (b) do you find out first how their own bookings are for the period, and assess

168

how much they might need your business; (c) tell them you are sorry for wasting their time, but someone else has got your business; (d) give them the impression that you do a great deal of business with their hotel chain all over the world and their price had better be good as a result?

Score   **Score**

_____   _____

            Before reading chapter.   *After reading chapter.*

_____   _____

Q.4   *You name all the best features of the competitor's offerings to them. Do you do this:*

            (a) All at once, along with the price you expect to pay; (b) bit by bit, getting their agreement, and then asking for their price; (c) telling them this is a no-frills conference and the price is important to you, adding your demands after they've quoted their price; (d) let the conversation take its course naturally?

Score   **Score**

_____   _____

            Before reading chapter.   *After reading chapter.*

_____   _____

Q.5   *You never pay your bills earlier than 120 days if you can possibly avoid it. Do you:*

            (a) ignore this altogether unless they raise it; (b) tell them this honestly during the conversation; (c) tell them you expect them to abide by your normal terms and to talk with your accountant; (d) exchange better payment terms for a extra concession with 5% off.

Scores

It's quite easy to score an overall minus on these questions.

Above 14	Sharp you are. Do you do it for a living?
8–13	You could do this for a living.
0–8	You are too nice a person to make a really good living.
Minus score	People skin you, but they like you.

Price Bargaining Tactics | 12

You may think you can get through life fairly easily without worrying too much about the state of the hot-rolled coil market. To be told that a hot-rolled coil is a vital part of the engineering industry is not likely to do much for your adrenaline.

But if you know that a price war has broken out yet again among the sellers of hot-rolled coils, you might perk up a bit. Particularly if you have anything to do with cars or refrigerators; you will be interested because it means your product costs should go down.

Not for long though, if the steelmakers in Europe have their way. Europe's steel club, Eurofer, consists of the fifteen biggest steelmakers. Their chief executives don't like price wars because they'll all lose money and some will go broke. But steel is such an important element in any developed economy that national governments cannot allow their own steel companies to go broke; if they lose money, they must be supported by government subsidies. Governments can't do much about it, either, except to fire the chief executives of the steel companies, which is called in the trade, "Not renewing the contract." So steelmakers have a strong interest in eliminating price wars among themselves. And while they are cutting out price wars in hot-rolled coils, they had better do something about the ridiculous prices for light sections of steel used in construction, wire making and some machine tools, which are also being sold below cost. We are talking about the early 1980s. By the late 1980s, the war will be fought somewhere else, no doubt.

But it is not too easy to stop a price war even if you are big. The steelmakers know that steel prices collapse when the demand falls well short of supply. But how are they all going to agree to cut back their supply, if they are producing at 55% capacity? How is one of them going to persuade 14 other giant companies to reduce production in a situation like that? Not only that, but big as they are, those steelmakers don't control all the industry. There are many efficient independent companies outside of Eurofer, and sometimes those companies have much lower overhead. If the giants cut back, the independents can move in—and they'll often make a profit even on the cut prices. Not only that, but if the steelmakers raise their prices for hot-rolled coils by the immediate and substantial amounts they talk about, many of their customers will buy cheaper supplies from overseas producers.

Finally, how would they monitor any agreement? It is all very well to make a deal between themselves, but how can they be certain one of the other companies will not be pressured by its government to keep its production high and to undercut the agreed-on prices by discounting?

All might look well on the surface—the list prices can be identical. But the hidden discounts to individual customers can be huge. And low production quotas agreed on by the producers are difficult to justify when they are putting their workers out of jobs as a result. Far from being dull and boring, hot-rolled coils are full of the stuff which drive people to the madhouse.

Practically all big deals are complex—"multifaceted." Price is only one of the issues to be agreed on, but it is often the central issue around which the rest of the deal revolves. So we have to look at the rest of the deal—there are hundreds of ways for buyers to get your price down, without complaining about your price. What they do is demand that your service go up.

Here is how to get what you want out of a complex deal. Remember, you are not fighting a battle, you are working toward a solution that is good for both companies—yours and his. That's the first rule. The second is to know what you want, and to be able to make a good guess at what he wants. Next, you must decide whether you are going to put everything you want in one package, or break it up into separate bits. Then you go for the exchange.

COLLABORATION IS THE SOURCE OF A GOOD DEAL

You cannot go in aggressively with your demands on the other man, if he does not want what you offer. You must present your offering in terms of its advantage to him. You must show him how much he needs what you offer; you must show him how unlikely he is to obtain your offer elsewhere. The unique properties of your offer must be stressed, and be shown to be important to him. In terms of the value for money that you propose, your offer must be a veritable star in a wilderness of competition. He will not show you he is excited by what you offer; this is part of his ritual to keep your expectations low.

But when you reach the stage where both of you are inclined to do business with each other, then search for joint benefits in the deal. Many times, deals are constructed as one-way moves. The gains of one side are paid for by the other side. If the buyer gets your price down and nothing else happens, then he has saved himself money, at your expense.

You need to escape from a situation of one-way gains and losses. You need to move into the area where both of you can do better.

For example, he might get your price down. But in exchange he agrees to pick up the product from your warehouse, and to pay you within seven days. Alternatively, you suggest a way of manufacturing for him in large batches to suit your production, and joint storage until he calls off the product, then you can give him a really special price. Alternatively, instead of his taking supplies from three different companies, you might show him the advantage of taking 80% of his requirement from you, which will earn him the maximum quantity discount. That leaves 20% to another supplier and provides him with the security of supplies he needs. And it cuts out a third supplier altogether. The first principle of exchange is to search for collaboration, rather than to engage in conflict.

Note: *The best deal is a deal with adequate profit for both sides.*

SETTING THE OBJECTIVES

Next, and most important, you must know what you want from him and you
must put that up against what you think he wants from you. List all the things
you offer him, together with the price you want. Rank them in order of importance to you—certain things you *must* have, such as standard specification,
or prompt payment, or your price objective. In addition, there are things you
would *like* to have, such as an order of much larger volume. And you would
like to try for a higher price. Perhaps you would also like to get cash up front—
who wouldn't? It's not always impossible, but you have to trade in the demand
somehow. And in dealing, if you don't trade it in and ask for it, then you
certainly will not get it.

Then set out his priorities—what you think he will demand from you. What
must he have, what do you think he would like to have? He is going to try to
get it all, if he can, and you must work out what you think he will settle for,
and what you think he will try for.

Break up what you offer into bits. If your terms are 60 days, then realize
that you don't have to give 60 days away immediately; say 30 days payment
instead. He will press you for 60 days. You can agree to it after an argument,
in exchange for something from him. If you give free servicing and maintenance,
separate them. Ask him if he wants it. If he does, then what can he give you
in return?

There may be bits in your package that you normally take for granted and
offer to everyone. There may also be other things that you can do for him that
he wants once you mention them. Many of those things will cost you only a
little. But they might be of considerable importance to him.

One large advertising client wanted a particular copywriter and visualizer to
work as a team on their account. They felt the creative work of the two would
be worth a fortune to them. So they asked the agency that employed the two
to handle their account. They did not disclose that a condition of the deal was
the inclusion of these two. Early on in the discussions, they indicated that the
agency's creative work was probably not good enough and showed signs of
walking away. The top two were then wheeled out and the client's interest
apparently returned. The agency gained the account, after many hours of debate
about the size of the fee the client would pay. The client secured a good financial
deal with a small fee. The agency never realized that the principal condition for
the client all the time was the appointment of the two creative people. The client
secured that concession early on in the deal, put it in his pocket and then put
the pressure on the price.

Many of the things you want from them, and they want from you, cannot
be quantified. You might want efficient order processing, and few last minute
rushes. They might want absolute realiability; if you say you are going to do
something, then you must be trusted to do it.

Such things cannot be quantified. But they can be listed and traded into the

Figure 12.1
Preplanning the deal

1 Objectives:
  Like to have
  Must have
  Don't want

2 Your priorities

3 What will he want?

4 What can he give us in exchange?

5 What concessions are of *most value* to him and of *least cost* to us?

package. You can offer reliability, perhaps by offering personally to look after their business. Would they want that? (If you have done the deal well, then they will want that.) Well, fine, you are willing to handle their business personally, but they must give you direct access to their people and keep to a regular plan for meetings. Their order office must work smoothly with yours—and so on.

BUNCHING OR BREAKING

Now that you know all the things you want from him, and can guess at the things he wants from you, you will have to decide whether to bunch or break. Bunching is when you bundle together in a package all the things you want from him, announce them up front and tell him your offer. You try and secure agreement on the lot. (You can bunch *elements* of the deal without putting in the whole lot.)

Or you can break up the deal into small bits and trade them one by one. You secure agreement on each principal bit before you move on. You might deal with individual products in that way. It is difficult to make more than two or three major-product presentations in any one interview. But you cannot bunch things together unless the other person understands all the components you are offering. Very often, whether you should bunch or break is clear from the situation. If he is generally ignorant about what you propose, then you must take him through it bit by bit.

But he also can bunch or break up his demands. Once you have told him your offer, he can think about it a bit and then come at you with a complete package that includes everything he wants; he can then offer you a price that seems to be "take it or leave it." A very experienced buyer, knowledgeable in your field, who understands the absolute limit of what he can get on a deal, may use this technique. What should you do? You should separate it and break it up into bits as far as you can. Take the main item, and press him precisely on his requirements there. Then take the next. Cost each item separately as you go; your cost accounting will show a higher price than he has offered you. That is the area where you must trade. If he won't raise his price to you, then you must leave something he wants out of the package. That's dealing.

A buyer will use this technique if he knows the field very well, or if he wants to frighten you out of demanding a high price.

Most buyers do not know the limit of all the concessions they can get. They test each supplier in turn. They try and secure a general commitment from the salesman on the issue of price, without themselves being committed to buying at that price. Then they go in with their big demand first, and try to get the salesman to agree to that. Then they move in with their next, and so on down the list.

Having committed himself on price, but not having secured the buyer's agreement to buy, the salesman finds he is being chipped at, bit by bit, until all his discretion to offer extra services or to make price reductions has been taken away from him, until finally he says "no."

The tactic to use here is again the opposite one. If they are bunching, you should break it up; if they are breaking, then you should bunch your side of the deal. Do not become committed to your lowest price early on. Find out what else they want in the deal first. Explain that you can only price the deal when you know everything they want from you. Then you bunch all their demands together and price the whole package.

The strategies of breaking and bunching do not solve all the problems of dealing with skilled buyers. But they mean you will lose less often.

Finally, you will get to a situation where you are going to exchange the things they want from you for the things you want from them. You will be able to see the items that link together nicely. Like goes with like for the most part; and high value goes with high value. Most of the linking issues will be obvious. If they want you to waive your minimum order requirement for product A, then they will have to deliver a full vehicle. Could their orders on A be linked to a higher volume deal on B which would make up the load? If they want to put their own quality control inspectors on your production line, they will have to guarantee by contract to take the entire output on that line, and so on. Yes, you will secure a leasing deal for them on the equipment they buy from you, but it will have to include a small insurance policy premium so that, if for some reason they default on the charges, the whole deal will be paid up immediately. And so on. This is the lovely, creative part of dealing. Before you can get to it, however, you must both want something from the other, and your respective power must be more or less equal. If one of you does not want the other, there is no point in looking for such exchanges.

Figure 12.2
Bargaining: points to look for

Collaborative bargaining	:	Not conflict bargaining
Set your objectives	:	Don't play it as it comes
Sort out the bits you want	:	Don't do all the giving
If he breaks up his demands	:	You don't bunch them
If he bunches his demands	:	You don't break them
If you...then we...	:	Don't give it away

HOW TO TIE STRINGS

Be careful how you link the issues. If you are going to make a concession on price or discount, be sure something comes back the other way. Otherwise you will be left offering them the lower price, having forgotten to hook it up to something. The way to do this is to start with the two magic words: "IF YOU..." When you are linking issues, if you get into the habit of putting those two words up front, followed by what you want from them you will have set a condition on what you are going to give them. You can then go on in the last part of the sentence to say "THEN WE..."

"If you can get the order to us by Monday, confirmed in writing, then we can get it to you for your Thursday production, guaranteed." "If you introduce this question to your colleagues in the association, so that all the group business, which is worth $250,000 a year, comes to us then we will give your company an extra rebate of 1½% on the business we do together." "If you cut down the branch of your tree overhanging our kitchen window, we'll stop our cat from terrorizing your canary." "If you hand over your wallet, I'll put this gun away."

SUMMARY

The best deals are those with profit to both sides. Deals where one side loses are unhealthy and rarely stick. So it pays to work toward collaboration where both sides can win more of what they want.

But in any deal, there will always be an element of one side seeking to gain an advantage at the expense of the other side. Getting a supplier to reduce this price, and offering nothing extra in exchange is one such means, and most frequently used by buyers. They may carry out a plan to do this quite deviously, and it pays to be on guard most of the time to avoid being caught in a buyer's trap.

A difficult buyer is not usually one who sounds pugnacious or makes extreme demands. His manner, on the contrary, might be warm and accommodating, seeking to relax the sales executive. Typically, he will try to get the seller's price down early in the conversation.

He might argue fiercely over it, and then move on to other matters, coming back to the price later. His objective is to secure a commitment from the salesman without himself making a commitment to buy. It can happen that he might not argue too fiercely over the price, having gotten it down, because his principal objective might be to secure some other large concession as part of the package he wants. The value of the concession might be more than he can expect to obtain on price, so he might soften his price argument and introduce his big demand early.

Throughout this, it is important for the seller to avoid being caught in the trap of granting all the concessions one way. The seller should have a list of what he wants and should match it against his thoughts about what the customer might want. Breaking up the deal into component bits is a very important part of the dealing process. Many sellers become bored with the prospect of a long haggle over the details, and try to clear up the outstanding issues in a bundle. They concede the small things in the deal without thinking. Then they approach the end of the conversation only to find they have given away all of their cards, and the buyer still has not committed himself to the deal. It is a major error of selling strategy; one to be avoided at all costs.

To avoid it, simply don't name the price up front. You can float an idea of it if you like, but leave yourself plenty of room. Every time he makes another demand, you must cost it, out loud. When he has exhausted all his demands, then you can add up the individual costs of what he wants from you. The total of those costs will be much higher than the price you would have quoted him firmly at the start. Now you are free to give him the total price, and then deal from there.

Assess in advance what he is likely to want. Be careful to tie strings to any deal you offer him. Make your offer conditional upon his doing something for you in return. And remember one of the golden rules from a previous chapter: The biggest profit comes from selling large volume at a sensible price. Often, he is in a position to give you more volume business; that's what you want from him in exchange for what he wants from you.

Organizing for Pricing Decisions | 13

This is the free chapter!

Before reading the chapter, complete the answers to these questions in the spaces on the left-hand side. Then without looking at the answers, read the chapter. Finally, complete the answers again, making any changes you think fit. Score both sets of your answers. This tells you how much the chapter has affected your opinion. Scores are at the end of the book (p. 204).

HOW GOOD A COMPANY PRESIDENT ARE YOU?

Q.1 *You are zone general manager for a car firm. A distributor of yours has upset the local market and all your other distributors in the area by his vigorous price cutting on new models. He is not supposed to do that. On the other hand, he has sold a lot of cars for you. You are to see him shortly. Will you:*

(a) Slap his wrist for being naughty but let him know you are not really bothered; (b) ignore the whole thing; (c) play the heavy; after all you have your other distributors to protect; (d) encourage him all you can?

Score   **Score**
___   ___

        Before reading chapter.   *After reading chapter.*

___   ___

Q.2 *A certain farmer whom you call on waits until you have left his farm, having given him a good price for high-energy cake to feed his calves, and then telelphones your sales director for a better price. The sales director usually gives him an extra discount. When you hear about it, do you:*

(a) Say that's the sales director's privilege; (b) say as long as you get the business it does not matter how; (c) say the practice is damaging to the organization and is undermining the sales force; (d) suggest similar powers of discretion over discounts for the salesman?

Score   **Score**
___   ___

        Before reading chapter.   *After reading chapter.*

___   ___

Q.3   *Which is the most reliable source of market information about prices:*

(a) Your salesmen reporting back from customers; (b) competitors' price lists; (c) market research among customers; (d) press reports; (e) a bit of each of them added together?

Score   **Score**

‾‾‾‾‾‾‾

                  Before reading chapter.   After reading chapter.

‾‾‾‾‾‾‾

Q.4   *You are the president of a supermarket chain and Christmas is coming in eight weeks. Toys sell well then. Toy firms are flat on the floor and will make special deals. Would you try and choose this time to:*

(a) Cut the price of toys deeply, and advertise it widely, using extra discounts from your suppliers; (b) harden the price of toys and raise your margins; (c) take normal margins, squeezing suppliers just the same; (d) leave toy promotion to your branch managers, who know their markets?

Score   **Score**

‾‾‾‾‾‾‾

                  Before reading chapter.   After reading chapter.

‾‾‾‾‾‾‾

Q.5   *Would you expect to have a strategic decision, such as that on the full-scale price promotion of toys in the supermarket, be taken by:*

(a) Senior management; (b) branch and unit managers; (c) the buyers; (d) the marketing team?

Score   **Score**

‾‾‾‾‾‾‾

                  Before reading chapter.   After reading chapter.

‾‾‾‾‾‾‾

Q.6   *In an ideal world, would you like your field salesmen to:*

(a) Have no discretion at all over price; (b) have a little discretion over discounts but not much; (c) have complete discretion but know how to use it; (d) have a lot of discretion but jeopardize their commission if they use it?

Score   **Score**

‾‾‾‾‾‾‾

                  Before reading chapter.   After reading chapter.

‾‾‾‾‾‾‾

Q.7   *In the long run, what should you base your pricing policy on:*

(a) A profit objective; (b) a sales objective; (c) a market-share objective; (d) a maximum-growth objective?

Score   **Score**

———   ———

               Before reading chapter.   *After reading chapter.*

———   ———

Scores
Above 21   Ask the boss to make you director of pricing.
14–20   You ought to be advisor to the director of pricing.
8–13   You'll never make it as director of pricing. Have you thought about being managing director instead?
7 or less   It's good that we don't sell the book on sale or return.

Organizing for Pricing Decisions | 13

This extra chapter is free!

If you are a manager, you are not going to like this chapter. We have put it at the end so that if you want to lend the book to your boss, you can tear out this chapter first.

If you happen to be the world's greatest expert on advertising, just mention the fact at any party, and you will find yourself surrounded by other people equally "expert." Madame de Pompadour, the finest courtesan of her day, claimed that all the women in France secretly believed they were better than she was at making love. Men will always believe that given the right encouragement, they could run the mile or climb Mt. Everest with the best of them.

Everyone reading this book starts off by being the world's best pricer; the only thing is that the rest of the world has not yet recognized the fact. The book has readers seeking to confirm their own prejudices. As they read it, the head nodders knew they were right all along. The head shakers have not even read this far. I hate to write this, but it has got to come out sooner or later.

Your company should not delegate its pricing decisions down the line.

There you are, it is said. Out in the open at last. Only chief executives can be expected to agree with the sentiment.

In a small organization with few people, the chief executive can control prices easily. He chips a bit here, he pushes a bit there, he juggles the whole thing around according to the market, and he finds a way of making money. It is a very sensitive and flexible decision-making routine.

As the business grows, he employs other people. The business becomes less sensitive, less flexible. The business is bigger, more complicated. The product range is wider. The business serves a wider range of markets. Cost accounting is too complicated to be carried in the head. The business ends up with an organizational structure. There are committees. Departments get in the way of each other. Salesmen can't get a hearing in the higher reaches of power. Cost accountings abound, apparently to help people make profitable decisions; when the cost accountings don't turn up with the right answer, people don't trust them. (When they do—the one people wanted in the first place—no one ever mistrusts them.)

So the further the business organization removes itself from the market, the less sensitive it is to the marketplace. And that has a direct impact upon pricing decisions.

Separate the analysis from the decision.
The original chief executive with his small business is actually doing three things.

He is sensitive to the market and is able to analyze the situation quickly. Many events occur in the market to which he will not respond. But when his analysis tells him to move, he moves by making a pricing decision. Finally, he monitors the results—not in any calculated way, but by feeling the way the business grows when he makes pricing decisions.

The first requirement is analysis—and that should be separated from the pricing decision. The closer the analysis gets to the marketplace, the better—so the top salesmen must be an important part of the feedback. And the more that market feedback can be verified by independent evidence, assessed by experts inside the company, the better. Speed is essential; but so is accuracy and relevance.

We have spent a considerable amount of time in persuading readers not to rely on what the buyers say for their market information. What we mean is—treat such evidence with care, and try at all costs to obtain substantiating evidence. Three buyers giving the same explicit information about a competitor's price is reasonable evidence—provided that the information is reported by three different salesmen who have not spoken to each other first.

A lot of people have a vested interest in bending the information coming back to a company from the field. The person with the greatest interest is the buyer—but the salesman may also want a decision turned in a particular way and he is an expert persuader. If he wants a particular decision and he is good at the job, he will fix it so the company produces the results he wants. So all such information needs verification, proof, checking and independent evidence.

Salesmen can be very good researchers, provided that you ask them to verify observable things—how big is the factory, how many vehicles are there in the competitor's yard at start-up time, and so on. But they are poor at reporting opinions and judgment. They are trained to manipulate and use information, not to assess it scientifically.

The first thing to do organizationally is to ensure that someone has the responsibility for monitoring the market. That is an expert job in its own right. He will use published research evidence (particularly from the trade press); he will use market research evidence where it is appropriate; he will collect competitors' price lists; he will interview and screen newly hired personnel from competitive companies. He will assess the reports from the field; he will ask salesmen for specific information on a selective basis, and will check one piece of information against another from a different source.

He or she can be a committee, and that committee can also assess company cost factors. Material cost changes, distribution cost changes, labor cost changes need to be fed into the analysis. Profitability needs to be studied, item by item, product by product, market by market. Total sales volume, overhead costs and budgets need to be compared. All of that will help pricing decisions, and all the information needs to come together at some expert point down the line.

But the most important data will also be the hardest to collect, the hardest to believe and the hardest to verify: the data from the market. Information about

Figure 13.1
Participants in pricing progress

FUNCTION	WHY HELPFUL
General management *Marketing* (sales, research, advertising, product manager, middlemen)	1 Makes pricing decisions. Has primary responsibility for recommending price changes and administering prices. 2 Has knowledge of buyers' needs, attitudes toward company and competitors, and buying behavior. 3 Provides data on company, distribution channels, markets, industry and economic situation. 4 Provides data on competitive prices, reactions, products, strategies, and capabilities. 5 Tracks sales trends and measures market acceptance and reactions to different prices. 6 Makes estimates of probable volume. 7 Schedules marketing costs for existing and new products.
Controller/Finance (accounting)	1 Determines effect of required investments on working capital. 2 Calculates pricing formulas to net a desirable profit and return- on-capital. 3 Periodically checks validity of, and yield from, current prices. 4 Sets standards and estimates costs. 5 Does cost, payback, break-even, and performance analyses for each product. 6 Does risk analyses. 7 Reports findings regularly to product and sales managers.

Production/engineering	1 Assists in establishing standard costs as a basis for establishing other pricing levels.
	2 Anticipates and analyzes production difficulties that may affect prices.
	3 Suggests contingency budget for unexpected costs.
	4 Compares product benefits, applications, premiums received by buying, utility, production economics, quality, and service with competitive products.
	5 Analyzes and suggests potential economies of scale.
Legal counsel	1 Assures compliance with pricing and antitrust legislation.
	2 Assures proper trademark and patent control.
Public relations	1 Measures or estimates effects of price changes and policies on attitudes of customers, distributors, and government.
	2 Measures or estimates image and prestige levels of company and competition.
Economist	1 Determines probable sensitivity of demand to price levels under consideration.
	2 Monitors state of general economy and its probable effect on current and future price.
Pricing specialist	Involved in all of the above. Coordinates and integrates inputs from above functions.

competitive bids for big volume business from key accounts is central to pricing decisions.

The data are needed to assist in the analysis and to help the company meet pricing objectives. The analysis of the information should not be handled within the financial function, because that will skew information toward cost factors. For a similar reason it should not be part of the sales department. The most effective place for it is in a market research section within the marketing department; but if it is contained there, then the financial representation in the analysis should be strengthened.

PRICING OBJECTIVES

Pricing objectives break down into several components and serve two general aims: short-term tactical moves and long-term strategic moves.

In the short run, pricing objectives can be set against:

meeting existing competition
discouraging new competition
securing key accounts
recovering cash rapidly
attracting new customers, distributors, agents
using spare capacity
trimming off overfull demand.

In the longer run, pricing objectives can be set against:

return on sales; return on assets
stabilizing price and margin relationships
realizing target market share
strategic pricing in different markets
keeping competition out of key markets.

With such short-term and long-term objectives in view, it is clear that the company needs different levels of authority for different kinds of pricing decisions. To adjust a specific customer's price in order to sell him more volume and to keep out competition is a decision that can be taken further down the line than a decision of much more consequence to the future of the company— for example, to go for growth by cutting the level of gross margin hoping that bigger sales overall will more than compensate for the price cut. This latter is clearly a top management decision to be taken very cautiously, if at all.

The trouble is that many companies do not have a formal hierarchy of decision-making responsibility. So buyers exert pressure on the sales department which gives in, bit by bit, and gradually the effect is to lower the total company gross profit across the board. In that way, a company gets into trouble through its margins being too low, without any decision to that effect having been made at all.

That is why pricing decisions should not be passed down the line. Special discounts offered to customers should first be assessed by management for approval. A decision to offer a tactical discount can only too quickly spread like wildfire around the market.

For evidence of that, just look at the discounts you offer your customers for bulk drops in delivery. When those discount terms were set up, you made a financial calculation that you could be sure of earning back some savings with fewer drops in bigger deliveries through larger loads. But perhaps you made the mistake of publishing those discounts—if you tried to change them now, you could be in trouble, even though the original cost factors have altered.

Just ask your management accountant to give you an analysis of your drop costs today, at today's fuel prices, compared to your discount structure. You'll find you are hopelessly out on your drop discounts. You are giving away too much to some, and not enough to others. While you can always give away more than you do, try regaining some from the unprofitable drops. (You can alter discounts when the growth comes back into the market, when your demand is strong and no one has enough of the product to supply. Remember those happy days? That's when you will be strong enough to alter your discounts.)

Transfer pricing
Another major organizational problem is the price that one division charges another for the work it does. In decentralized companies with interdependent business, it can be a most difficult problem, one leading to a great deal of internal strife and, unless handled carefully, a loss of profit-earning capacity. It is a well-known feature of many large multiproduct organizations that the most difficult buyers they have to sell to are those working for their own company.

The basic principles of sound transfer pricing are fairly clear:

1 The prices and costs should be allocated in such a way as to reflect an accurate measure of efficiency. One division's profits should not be so vastly inflated by favorable pricing that other division's profits are severely depressed.
2 Transfer prices should not allocate a greater profit to a division than it would be capable of earning on its own, without the synergistic effect of working with another part of the group.
3 Sound transfer prices should ensure that any action taken to increase the company's total profit does not decrease the division's profit.

Where goods are passed from one division to another in the form of raw materials or finished products, there are three pricing systems in common use. These are as follows.

Paying the market rate for the product
This means the buying division is paying full cost for the product more or less at the rate it could obtain outside the firm. The difficulties are obvious. The division may pressure the company to allow it to buy outside, thereby depriving another division of the income; the buying division may feel resentful that the full profit has been obtained by another division and may increase demands for a higher level of service. The supplying division, finding itself with a most profitable customer within its own group, will lack the incentive to develop business outside, which is harder to obtain and less profitable to serve.

Paying the marginal cost of the goods only
This has the reverse effect, in that only the direct cost of the product and limited overhead are taken by the supplying division, which then has a tendency to drop the level of service and generally become resentful and difficult to deal with. In an extreme case, if the supplying division has no other outlet for its production, then it can be made to look so unprofitable that the company can consider closing it. That would be a poor company decision since, apart from the loss of company contribution, the buying division would now have to pay full market rates for its product.

The most equitable system should involve a sharing of the combined profits between the two divisions as a result of the synergy. For example, the supplying division could take no net profit from the deal, and could pass on all the genuine savings in marketing, sales and distribution. Beyond that it could share some of its research and development charges and other central service charges with the buying division. That leaves the buying division with a product that is cheaper than it would be if purchased, and it leaves the supplying division with some overhead contribution from the business. The system can be operated with a general company discount applied to the normal sales price which might be 15% or more.

Where purchasing officers are contributing heavily to the profitability of their division, and resent having their hands tied by having to buy certain products from within the company, the company policy might allow them to purchase a proportion of their requirements from outside suppliers, perhaps up to 20%. That gives them some leverage on their own company suppliers, who are forced to compete for the business to some extent, and it gives them some experience of the marketplace. The competitive advantages of the practice may outweigh the loss of contribution from the business that goes to outside suppliers. Indeed, purchasing officers are often only too happy to come back to the intra-company supplier when they find they receive a poorer level of service from outside.

If a purchasing department can show that their overall profit contribution can be increased if they are allowed to buy a particular requirement outside— perhaps because of very favorable terms offered which more than outweigh the profit contribution to the supplying company—then the policy should allow them to be able to make out the case for the company management's final decision.

THE PRICING DECISION

The decision on margins as a whole should be set by general management. A basic requirement of the business should be to improve efficiency and to reduce the unit cost over a period of time, in order to maintain the gross margin. Another should be to trade prices effectively in the market.

Within the general framework of pricing policy, the marketing management team can now set prices for products and markets based on market data; policy guidelines on costs and margins, and management accounting information. Some multiproduct companies have a management accounting function built into their marketing department structure, and that is an ideal system because it brings together the costing skill with the market analysis, without destroying the element of "feel" or intuition which is such a vital part of the pricing process.

Such a system can now be used also to set prices for large key accounts. It is the modern practice for companies to reveal their product profits to the sales force, and even more modern to aquaint negotiators for key accounts with the profitability of the business they do. I do not totally endorse this view; if I were a national accounts negotiator I would not want to know the precise details of the profit on every deal. I would want to know that A is more profitable than B, and that C is more profitable than D. I would want some information on the cost of delivery, or special promotions. But if management gave me all the detailed information, I would become a hostage to any buyer who wants to drive me down to a bottom price in exchange for high volume. I want to know when to say "no"; if there is more to come, I can come back with it later. If I have full discretion on price, the buyer will sense it because I will be slow to respond with horror to his big demands if I figure I can make a marginal contribution out of his offer.

> Note: *In some countries of the world, if you help an opponent of the regime, it is best if you do not know his name. Because if the government catches you, they'll get the name from you one way or another. But if you don't know it, then you can't tell them. It's the same with buyers and your bottom limit price.*

Should discounts be published?
No. Let them argue for them. Just publish the price list; negotiate the rest. You know the routine. If you have to do something for them, such as giving them a discount, then they must do something for you.

Should salesmen be taught how to handle price?
Yes. Without a doubt, a fortune is given away daily when it is not necessary to do so. If the salesmen are taught how to handle price, they will be firmer on the issue and will not lose any business as a result. Actually, they will gain

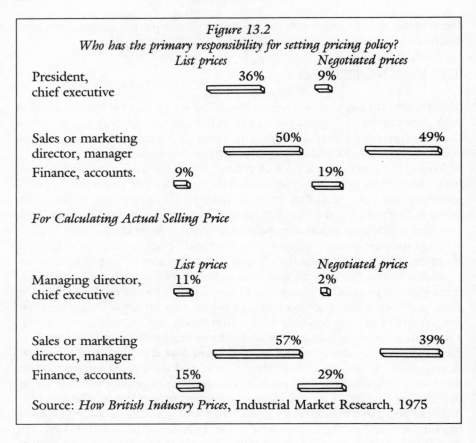

Figure 13.2
Who has the primary responsibility for setting pricing policy?

	List prices	Negotiated prices
President, chief executive	36%	9%
Sales or marketing director, manager	50%	49%
Finance, accounts.	9%	19%

For Calculating Actual Selling Price

	List prices	Negotiated prices
Managing director, chief executive	11%	2%
Sales or marketing director, manager	57%	39%
Finance, accounts.	15%	29%

Source: *How British Industry Prices*, Industrial Market Research, 1975

business, because they will know how to trade up the volume for a lower price.

If the salesmen have no leeway at all on pricing decisions, but must refer to their managers on every extra discount, they will be the most effective. They will sell on nonprice features of the product and cannot be bargained down. If the manager allows them to go a little further on price here and there, they should be taught how to land the business while giving away as little of the extra discount as possible. Most men give most of the extra discount away most of the time. "Oh, are you going to pay me in cash then?" says the salesman to the farmer, surprised. "Well then, that'll get you an extra discount of 2½%." Salesmen call it customer service. Accountants call it giving money away.

> Definition: *The technical description of this is: "Buying back the business after you've sold it."*

If the salesman has a lot of discretion on price, then it is even more important for him to know how to deal properly. So, on every count, salesmen must be taught how to sell price.

Many salesmen must carry some discretion around with them because they operate in industries where it is expected—selling earthmoving equipment to plant leasing operators, for example. Or they sell to very high volume users, where the extra purchasing power demands extra special prices. But be sure you teach them how to negotiate properly.

Should there be discount discretion up the line?

Yes. The general principle of allowing little discretion should be followed as closely as the business will allow. Salesmen will argue with it furiously and will not see that it is in their own interests. No discretion, or as little as possible, for those selling in the field. A little sweetener can be allowed by first line supervisors. A small percentage discount, or better still, a promotional allowance, can be granted by the area manager; and a bigger one granted by the regional manager. Above that level, special deals need to be worked out for key accounts and costed separately. Although I do not generally like the idea of turning a key-accounts salesman into a walking financial calculator, it is vital to keep the profit information somewhere, where key accounts are concerned. Where? With the salesman's superior. So everyone up the line has a little discretion to move prices, but within a general framework fixed by top management.

The final and most important point about all this is: never let the chief himself offer the extra discount to the customer, even if he attends the meeting. Always, always, the offers must be passed to the customer by the executive handling the account. The chief must never override his executive's authority and control.

Monitoring price changes

Every time a price change takes place, either up or down, there should be a preliminary statement of purpose and a sales forecast. The results should then be compared with the forecast, and variances explained.

The purpose of this exercise is not to prove whether the decision was right or wrong, nor to allocate praise or blame, but simply to provide evidence of results when price changes take place.

Thus, a body of knowledge is buuilt up which is most valuable as a source of management evidence when later price changes are made. It is a vital discipline to prepare a price-objective statement and a sales forecast, because they take everyone through the logic of the move from and stop irrational moves from being made. Evidence of the results, market by market, accumulates quickly and should be monitored immediately after the change. If it is not, you will not be able to separate it from the resulting effects of other changes you made to your marketing approach.

Individual discounts granted by different salesmen should also be monitored separately and the results made known to the sales force. There will be much argument on the figures and much special pleading, but the effect will remain the same. The field force will see how much each of them is being made to depart from the list price, and each of them will try that much harder to get off the top of the heavy discounter list.

Figure 13.3
Don't delegate too much discretion

In 1977, 50% of the members of the American Surgical Trade contributed profit and loss balance sheet information, plus a description of their marketing characteristics to the organization, so an analysis could be made of the performance of member companies. 108 companies were involved in the research, one of the purposes of which was to study the implications of giving salesmen discretion on price. In 29% of the sample, sales personnel had no authority whatsoever to deviate from list prices and published discounts (except with management approval). In 48% of the sample, some pricing latitude was permitted at the field-sales level. In 23% of the sample, considerable discretion was allowed to the field salesmen; the only control was that commissions were set against the gross margins earned. The lower the gross margin, the more the salesman's commission was penalized. The table shows the results:

Degree of pricing authority delegated to sales force	Gross margin earned	Sales per sales representative	Return on assets (%)
Low pricing discretion	1.05	0.87	11.8
Medium pricing discretion	0.98	1.21	10.5
High pricing discretion	0.94	0.76	9.6

The figures are compared to a normal index figure of 1.0, except for return-on-assets figures, which are shown as normal average percentages for the group as a whole.

The highest level of sales per representative was obtained for those companies giving their sales executives a moderate level of discretion on price.

(Interestingly, the study indicated a relatively low level of sales per representative when representatives have a great deal of discretion.) But the highest contribution per representative was earned by those without any leeway on price. That finding was also reinforced by the figures for the return on capital, which was also the highest for those companies.

So, if you want to sell more, give your salesmen some, but not much, discretion on price. But if you want to make more money, then don't give them any discretion. That forces them to sell the quality, which is what you want anyway, isn't it?

Question: What are you in business for — a lot of sales, or a lot of profit?

Finally, the special discounts and promotions given to large accounts, specifically in exchange for volume deals or other effort on their part, also need to be monitored to see that the large accounts keep their side of the bargain. An extra 1½% rebate can often be given away in anticipation of future orders, and later the forecast orders do not quite reach target. That needs careful watching. Much better to offer the big-volume discount as a rebate afterward. Then you can be sure they have met their targets; meanwhile you have improved your cash position until you pay the rebate. At a credit cost of over 1% per month, that can add up to a tidy sum in saved interest on the rebate.

SUMMARY

Try to give your people down the line as little discretion to vary price as possible. They'll have to have some—but make sure they always make the customers struggle for the discount. The best way to do that is to make sure *they* have to struggle for permission to give. They won't like being strapped down, but it is the only safe way.

Make sure you have a good analysis of the market, of the competition and of your costs and profits. Make sure that the analysis comes together in the same place at the same time; and be sure that doubtful data from the market place are verified independently. Sales information is a fair source provided you don't believe everything the buyers tell you; check the information using several different people.

Strategic pricing decisions relating to market-share goals or margin goals should be reserved for top management, using recommendations from below.

Be sensible about transfer pricing, and make sure that savings are shared between the buying and selling divisions within the same company; otherwise resentment breaks out because one division feels the other has the advantage. If you must load the price to a division because you want to take offshore profits then give them a token allowance in their annual performance assessments.

Make certain any discount given to a customer is given to him by the salesman handling the account, and not by the salesman's manager. The manager himself should be much more difficult on price than the salesman when both are in front of the customer. This way, the customer wants to deal with the salesman in the future, not with the manager.

So make everyone work hard for the things they feel they must give away, and publish to the field force the total amounts given to the customers by the field salesmen.

Have a pricing policy agreed on by top management, known down the line and acted upon. Base it ultimately on some notion of a suitable profit return on investment. That will translate into an average gross profit return across the board needed for a given volume of sales. The "average" now needs to be modified because you'll need to earn higher margins on some product ranges to compensate for the lower margins on other product ranges. Add this requirement to the need for new-product development, match it to market potential, add in the market and competitive pricing data, and you'll have a concoction that will delight the writers of your books and the marketers of your products when they come together to set prices and discounts.

Answers to Questions

CHAPTER 2

Q.1   They are all very likely, with the exception of (*c*) (very unlikely) and (*f*) (either perhaps or very unlikely). Score 1 for each correct answer.

Q.2   All these factors are important, but principally you must find out first what is making money and what is not. So (*d*) is the first line of attack, score +5. (*a*) or (*b*) or (*e*) score +3. (*c*) scores +1. (By itself the figure is meaningless. The others all give an indication of performance.)

Q.3   A great deal depends on your judgment of the company, the market and the competition, but on the evidence given, (*a*) is a disaster, score −5; you will be on your knees within a year. (*b*) is a good solution to keep in mind. At least you will stay profitably in business. Possibly a bit drastic at this stage. Score +4. (*c*) 0. (*d*) +5. You can still move to option (*b*) later. (*e*) +2. Too slow. Your problem is more ugent than this.

Q.4

  (*a*)   This is the most difficult and dangerous policy to pursue. Some do it successfuly, but their road is littered with failures. Score +1.
  (*b*)   You are unlikely to fail with this policy, but equally, you may not be an uproarious success. You could have a comfortable life. Score + 4.
  (*c*)   This can be a very successful policy, and is not as dangerous as it looks. Score +4.
  (*d*)   No, you must offer more than the market leaders if your price is the same as theirs. Most people adopt this policy, but that does not mean they find life to be easy or comfortable. Score +3.
  (*e*)   This is the way to sleep nights. In a comfortable bed. Score +5.

Q.5   (*a*)   +2
          (*b*)   +2
          (*c*)   −2   Very dangerous policy. Never make an investment whereby the entire business could be at risk if it fails.
          (*d*)   +5   It may be dull, but it makes the best sense.

Q.6   (*a*)   +5   The brand leader usually operates at prices around 7% above the average (as well as getting higher volume). This makes him the most profitable in cash profit terms.

193

(b)   +3

(c)   −1   The lowest price in the market does not usually sell the most.

(d)   0   He may be the highest in terms of the ratio of profit to turnover, or profit to capital employed. However, in terms of total profit generated, he will be beaten by the volume producers.

CHAPTER 3

Q.1   (a)   +1   Just because 81% do it the wrong way, is no reason for you to copy them.

(b)   +5   The market is a far more powerful determinant of prices than costs, so work within the natural flow.

(c)   +3   You will sell the product, but you will also miss opportunities this way.

(d)   −5   A shortcut to disaster and you know it, unless it's "trust your sales force" week.

(e)   0   How does he know about the market, the competition or the customers?

Q.2   (a)   +3   The OPEC cartel came into being because of the demand/supply position and the fact that oil production is concentrated in the hands of relatively few producers. Put simply, the world is gradually running out of its supplies of oil.

(b)   +1   If the world's oil prices were not so high, no one would try to get oil from the North Sea, because to do so, they would take a loss. The high production costs follow the price increase; they do not lead it.

(c)   +2

(d)   0

(e)   +5

Q.3   (a)   0

(b)   +2

(c)   0

(d)   +5   There is no other sensible way. What on earth have costs got to do with it?

(e)   +3   But even if you use this technique, you should still ask around the market first. Don't go blind.

Q.4   The correct sequence is shown in the question, i.e. (a) is first and (e) is last. All five correct, you can score +5. If you have the top three in the right order, you score +4. If you have the top three, but in the wrong order, you score $+3$. If you have the last two—(d) and (e)—in any of the top three positions, you score 0. Other answers $+1$.

Q.5 *(a)* $+5$ Swiss bankers buy gold, and they are not often wrong.
(b) 0 In 1971, it was \$35 an ounce; would you have said it was risky then?
(c) $+2$ Correct, but people buy gold in times of economic uncertainty.
(d) -2 Bit too eager!

Q.6 *(a)* 0
(b) 0
(c) $+2$
(d) or (e) $+5$. In the United States you would produce white eggs. But if you were an egg farmer in Britain, you would produce brown eggs. The preferred color is sold at a premium price in both markets even though the cost of production is identical for each color. There is no nutritional distinction, but many consumers believe there is.

CHAPTER 4

Q.1
Marginal pricing	Your neighbor (correct)
Standard cost pricing	Your wife
Product analysis pricing	You
Cost-plus-profit pricing	Your neighbor's wife

Four correct score $+5$
Two correct score $+2$
One correct score $+1$

Q.2 *(a)* Yes (correct Score $+1$ for each correct answer
(b) No
(c) Yes
(d) No
(e) Yes

Q.3 *(a)* No, you cannot.
(b) No, you would never have put the first wheel invented on the market if you costed in the time spent developing it.
(c) Sometimes.
(d) No. How is demand to be built into a standard formula?
(e) With sympathy for his problem, the answer is no. He is in the best postion to gather the data and to access the problem of allocating overheads.

(f) Yes, particularly if they gave them better market information in terms of forecasts.

(g) Sometimes. But sometimes you'll just cause the competition to lower theirs.

Score +2 for each correct answer

CHAPTER 5

Q.1 *(a)* −2

      (b) −5 They will pay anything to stay alive, of course, right up to the limit of what they and their families can afford. But how can you live with yourself?

      (c) +5

      (d) +1

Q.2 You could try them at $69.95 or $59.95 for a bit to see how they go, then reduce them later. Difficult to bring prices up if you start lower, but easy to bring them down. *(c)* and *(e)* score +5. *(a)* is $2 better than *(b)*, but both are poor because they go beyond "price points." Score *(a)* +1 and *(b)* 0. *(d)* scores −2. High fashion is not sensitive to price promotion.

Q.3 *(a)* 0

      (b) +1 A poor tactic because you will make your best customers look for bargains all the time if you are not careful. It might generate a bit of goodwill.

      (c) +1 Too rigid.

      (d) +5 Get rid of the lot altogether if you can, otherwise go for *(e)*.

      (e) +4 A classic technique. Relatively few, real loss leaders, but all of them promoted very heavily. But you will still attract price cutting to your market, and notice that you have to advertise your price cuts, as well as give the discounts away. It's expensive.

Q.4 *(a)* 0

      (b) +1

      (c) +2

      (d) +3

      (e) +5

Q.5 *(a)* 0

      (b) +2

(c) − 2
(d) + 5

CHAPTER 6

Q.1 (a) + 2 You can beat the world at tennis and golf and become a millionaire; but look at the competition!

(b) + 2 Sensible fellow, but lacks dedication to the aim.

(c) + 1 You'll want to join the civil service next.

(d) + 3 The energy is to be admired. But you'll use up all your time, and what millionaires need is time to be free to make money.

(e) + 2 Excellent idea. The aim is not mutually exclusive to that of being a millionaire. Indeed, why else might you want to be one?

(f) + 5 You knew it all the time. The sooner you start the better.

Q.2 (a) + 3

(b) 0

(c) + 4 Go for the unfamiliar when you can afford the losses.

(d) + 2 Difficult; you are leaving a lot to chance.

(e) + 1 It's attractive, but millionaires like some meaty volume in the market, and they thrive on competition.

Q.3 They are all important, and you would do a bit of each, but you would do best if you concentrate hard upon (c) + 4 points, and think less of (a) + 1 point—what's the hurry? (b) and (d) score + 3 points each.

Q.4 (a) Yes

(b) No

(c) Yes. Hong Kong. Fish where the fish are. And the fish in Hong Kong have money. All correct answers score + 3. Others zero.

Q.5 (a) 2 Your chances are not good.

(b) 2 Chances slightly worse if anything.

(c) 3 But people do sacrifice everything without making it.

(d) 1 It's a great shame our business society is all male-oriented. Even this book is written with the mental "map" of a reader who is male, and the author is *aware* that the problem of chauvinism exists.

(e) 4 Strangely, you've probably got the best chance with this experience.

(f)	2	Who wants to deal with you?
(g)	5	That's what you will be like—after you have made it.
(h)	3	You might know about people, but you've got to have the motivation yourself, too.

Q.6 Go for (b), (d) and (f). Score +3 for each correct one, zero for the others. Make something a bit different for people who have money and don't get yourself worked down by the middlemen.

CHAPTER 7

Q.1

(a)	+2	You can build expensive ones.
(b)	0	You'll be slaughtered on price.
(c)	+5	You must develop an edge and sell it hard.
(d)	+1	

Q.2

(a)	+2	Why discount? You've got nothing to compare it with.
(b)	+5	Don't be afraid of pricing up your competitive edge.
(c)	+1	Just give me a few moments in which to sell my shares in your company.
(d)	+3	It's unworkable on a mass market basis (but not with big contracts or with big bulk buyers).

Q.3

(a)	+4	But you are tying yourself to one maker, which reduces your own power a bit. It might be just a tiny bit strong altogether.
(b)	+2	If you are going to influence and control the market, then do it thoroughly. Exert your power over your suppliers too.
(c)	0	You not only lose power, you also lose money. You will lose your influence on the market in the end. Owners want to come to you for advice on their sails.
(d)	+5	It is not without its problems and you will have to maintain your hold on the suppliers for all time. But if you are successful, then they will come along with you.

Q.4

(a)	+4	Sensible.
(b)	+5	You may not be popular, but the word will get around the other owners. You are working in everyone's best interest (which happens to coincide with your own).
(c)	+1	Back to chaos You'll drag in the cheaper end of the market. And the price difference between secondhand boats and your new ones will show badly against you.

    (d) +3   You don't lack courage (or arrogance), but it is too strong. People don't like monopolistic buyers. How are you going to police it—by suing all the owners who break the contract?

Q.5 *(a)* 0   What are you, a printer or a boatbuilder?

    (b) +2   Better, but not much. This way you'll get down the basic unit price to the lowest level. But you don't want to sell on low price, do you?

    (c) +4   Much better.

    (d) +5   You have just added the finishing touch. Now that you have your competitive edge, and have controlled the design, you must make certain you keep control. Make it as difficult as possible for people to move outside you.

CHAPTER 8

The questions are so self-evident, that very good scores are demanded. The lowest score in each question is the best; but an extremely low score, in the area of *12* or less might show him to be rather inflexible. He is probably working in an industry where the quality content of what he offers is very high, and the prices are probably high also. Hence he will tend to avoid price fights as much as he can.

13–16 is a good healthy score. He will hold on and make sensible profitable deals most of the time. He might lose out here and there on the high volume but he would rather make the biggest profits than the biggest sales.

Above 25. He is a potential warmonger. He is probably used to working at the bottom end of some very tough markets and he works with some rapacious buyers. You know what? I hate to say it, but they are skinning him. Buy another copy of this book and give it to him.

CHAPTER 9

Q.1 *(a)* +3   Not bad, though the sales decline should make you think twice about a big rise in one jump. But you'll get away with it, probably.

    (b) 0   you can't afford to hang about.

    (c) +5   Yes, get the market used to price increasaes Make them normal.

    (d) −4   Don't advertise your beer as having a lot of body in it. If you try this kind of tactic with rival brewers, the body might be yours.

Q.2 *(a)* 0   Bit of a namby-pamby price leader. What's the matter, do meat pies bore you?

(b)   + 4   There's always the nice way and the nasty way. Try this nice way first.

(c)   + 3   Try this nasty way was second.

(d)   − 1   You'll never beat the small men out of the market. They would sooner starve than go out of business.

Q.3   *(a)*   + 1   Walking calculator, this fellow.

(b)   + 5   Well, the author is a marketing man too; and we have to hang together in times of crisis.

(c)   + 2   Read the chapter. Price increases should be nonnegotiable.

(d)   + 3   Too slow for a result, but his heart is in the right place (for a businessman that is).

For each one you get right, score + 2. If it's wrong by + 1 or − 1 score 1.

Q.4   *(a)*   + 5   I would still prefer to move with the others despite the attraction of *(c)*.

(b)   0   Crazy. The trade will think you've gone up twice. It will be very lonely when you do go up.

(c)   − 1   Price reductions must be advertised. Otherwise it's like blowing a kiss to a girl in the dark. You know what you are up to but she doesn't.

(d)   + 4   OK. I'll come along with you for the ride, but I think your chances of beating a fragmented market with a 10% price differential are remote.

Q.5   *(c)* is the only statement that is completely right. Score + 3 for it. 0 for others.

Q.6   Your problem is not raising the finance; you are not profitable enough. You have to move and to move fairly fast. 3 points each: *(a)* you are not going to like doing it, but it's taken too long already and the payoff is too far ahead; *(b)*neither you nor your staff will like this, but it must be done; *(h)*neither your suppliers nor your customers is going to like this, but your bank manager will. If you choose *(d)* − 3, you are a bit too concerned with your personal survival for comfort. *(c)*, *(e)*, *(g)* all + 1. *(f)* 0: unlikely to find one. *(i)* and *(j)* − 1: likely to damage your business.

CHAPTER 10

Q.1   By the time you have had all three questions answered you have established two limits—the lowest limit and the upermost limit. Now you are in a position to set your reserve price at, say $300 (below which he will take it out of the auction and sell it again, later). Don't leave the issue in his hands; and don't let him give you only a low-price expectation.

There are three limits you should set before any negotiation is started. There is:

the "best" deal you can get
the "worst" deal you will accept
the "likely" deal you will make.

The more you, or your agents or your subordinates are committed to those aims, the more likely you are to realize them.

Suppose you are now the auctioneer. Would you want to be committed by the seller to those three limits? Of course not. You want to press him down to expect the lowest limit, and to get the reserve price there. You would prefer to be unfettered by a price limit. If all your sellers were as difficult as this, you would have to work a great deal harder.

Q.2 In setting up the deal, you should generally ask for more than you expect to get, to give yourself a little bargaining room. There is nothing wrong in gently hinting at the Defense/State Department jobs; it puts the pressure on the President to settle for Treasury instead. With (c) you offer yourself as a hostage to fortune. (The President could indicate there is a good job going for you in Agriculture, and be willing to settle for Interior. It will be impossible for you then to take the President up to Commerce without a major fight.) (d) is a good position to hold, provided you get the timing right; it must be early on when the President needs your support badly. Make the President come to you until his/her offers are big enough.

Q.3 Getting the timing right is vital. The time to have a gentle exchange of views, and to come to an understanding from your point of view, is before the election campaign starts. When the President is making the appointments is far too late. On election night you will only create a row if you try it during the exhilaration of winning. Don't leave the timing to the President, otherwise you will be discussing it when the President is strong and you are weak, i.e. when the election is over and the President needs you less.

All of this is known as setting up the deal. Notice the use of gentle hints and exchanges, and using third parties instead of the principals. The expectations of each party should be signaled at the right time. The right time for one party is often the wrong time for the other.

CHAPTER 11

Q.2 Prices in the market have to do with perceived quality. The higher the perceived quality, the higher the price that will be paid, provided this quality is required by the buyer. Where the extra quality cannot be perceived by the buyer (he cannot touch it, or see it), he may be reassured that the higher quality exists *because* of the higher price. Price itself is a significant indicator of quality. (Not always a reliable indicator, but an indicator nevertheless.)

The cost of production of the license plates in the seminar game is identical. They add up to a few cents each. But the prices vary considerably. There is no doubt that even though the market is "imperfect" (i.e. not everyone knows all the information all the time, as in an auction), nevertheless the license plate with the perceived highest quality obtains the top average price. The license plate with the lowest perceived quality receives the lowest price.

The license plates are ranked in order of price. (*d*) IAM 007 is top at an average of $670. The rest run as follows:
(*a*) RU 1 $650;(*e*) RU 12 $500; (*b*) HIM 1 $375; (*h*) HIM 12 $300. The rest of the numbers are poor quality; (*g*) RU 123 $264; (*f*) HIM 123 $250; (*c*) MDX 227 $240.

So one principle emerges immediately: make sure your product or service has something perceptible and distinctive about it versus the competition, and hammer away at that difference. Called the Unique Selling Proposition, it remains a vital ingredient in price bargaining.

Q.3   (*a*) You would hold his attention to the better value for money that you offer compared to the higher priced competitor. You show him that you offer the same quality but at a saving of $400.

(*b*) Here you secure his agreement to the proposition that, if he is going to pay more, then he should expect something extra. (He will agree to this.) Then isolate your specific quality advantages (comparing specification to specification if necessary). Show him that the cost difference is only $66 per window, immediately recovered by the gain in capital appreciation in terms of the sale value of a house with double glazing installed.

(*c*) Just over $400 a window, or $8 a week for the first year for each window.

(*d*) If he keeps the house for 10 years it will have cost him only $250 a year or $5 a week; and he gets his money back and more when he sells the house.

(*e*) You need $400 for your extra quality against the low-priced competition; that's just over $1 a day extra for one year.

(*f*) What else could he buy for $1? Three cups of coffee a day?

(*g*) His fuel bills will be $150 per year greater, and rise each year with the cost of fuel. He will probably pay an unnecessary $2,000 in fuel costs in the next ten years alone; added to which he will lose the capital appreciation on the house price due to double glazing, which would mean a loss of another $1,500 perhaps. And if he decides to buy it in ten years time it will cost him twice as much then. He is not spending money at all. He is investing it for the future.

Incidentally, no one is suggesting that you should use all of these arguments. This would be much too glib, and would be offensive to the other party.

CHAPTER 12

Q.1   *(a)* +2
      (b) +1
      (c) −5
      (d) +5
      (e) −2

Get the competitive information first. Don't give away your whole hand, or they'll price it up. Don't tell lies about the booking because the deal won't stick if you do.

Q.2   *(a)* +5   Make sure they are relaxed enough to give you the information you want about their facilities. They'll also give you the lowdown on their rivals if you ask them nicely.

      (b) −3
      (c) +2
      (d) +3   No, what you want is to know what concessions you can get, as well as the price. But this is a fair tactic.

Q.3   *(a)* −5   You are a hostage to fortune if you do this.
      (b) +5   You can reconstruct parts of your deal to suit them, so if you find their pressure point you can squeeze them on the price.
      (c) +3   Not a bad tactic; it will weaken them but you will have to find a way of climbing down later and maintaining your integrity.
      (d) −2   It's too hard, too early. You have not gotten them excited enough about doing your business yet.
                You can use coercion only if the other party needs you.

Q.4   *(a)* +2   You could do this, but only if you are absolutely certain that you know everything they can offer, and you know their limit. If there is any doubt about it, you will have to chip away at them.
      (b) −4   If you do it this way, they'll just build up their price to the total of all your requirements.

    (c) +5   Yes, anchor the price first, then go in with your demands. You can ease up a bit on the price if they make too much difficulty. You just assume that the things you want in your conference package are included in their normal conference price package, don't you?

    (d) −2   No, hostage to fortune again. You might be dealing with a professional, so be prepared. Don't forget, there is money in this.

Q.5   *(a)* +1
       (b)   0
       (c) +2
       (d) +3   Provided the concession is worth more than the credit— you probably need a concession of more than 4% to break even against taking extended credit.

CHAPTER 13

Q.1   *(a)* +5   This is what I'd do.
       (b) +2   Hear no evil, speak no evil.
       (c)   0   The distributors don't pay your salary, the company does. The company makes cars to sell to people. The people pay the company money. If you don't sell cars, you don't get paid your salary. The equation is a simple one.
       (d) −2   Look, the salary isn't everything. The other distributors can make your life hard. You want an easy life *and* a salary.

Q.2   *(a)*   0   Nuts.
       (b) −1   It does matter how you get the business.
       (c) +5   Yes, take him to the cleaners. It's your account, not his.
       (d) +4   Yes, you can fight for it as long as you like, but if the company gives you such powers of discretion, then they lose Q.5. Lend them the book to read, will you?

Q.3   *(a)* +1   The quality varies depending on how manipulative the sales force is. How they manipulate you, the boss, that is.
       (b) +2   Yes, but you don't know the special deals.
       (c) +3   Well, everything helps but who answers questions on price truthfully, especially to market researchers?
       (d) +2   If you gave someone a really special low price, would you issue a press release about it? You'd buy Elastoplast for your press officer's mouth for a month.
       (e) +5   Right.

Q.4   *(a)* +5   That's what one British firm did on 154 of its 350 toy lines in November 1981, and thereby did half their annual toy sales in six weeks. They also brought in thousands of customers for the Christmas trade. It cost them nothing. Why? Because they squeezed the extra discounts out of their suppliers. Supermarkets know about price cutting; they get their suppliers to do it.

All other answers 0.

Q.5   *(a)* +5
        (b) +1
        (c) +2
        (d) +3   It's too important to delegate down the line.

Q.6   *(a)* +5
        (b) +2
        (c)   0
        (d) −1   The buyers will spot them coming a mile off.

Q.7   *(a)* +5
        (b)   0
        (c) +1
        (d) −5   After reading this far you *still* would? Ask someone for your money back. Not me, I've spent it.

Index